SHAKESPEARE

MACBETH

REVIEW QUESTIONS
AND ANSWERS

Bound to stay open

Publisher's Note

Otabind (Ota-bind). This book has been bound
using the patented Otabind process. You can
open this book at any page, gently run your
finger down the spine, and the pages will lie flat.

ABOUT COLES NOTES

COLES NOTES have been an indispensible aid to students on five continents since 1948.

COLES NOTES are available for a wide range of individual literary works. Clear, concise explanations and insights are provided along with interesting interpretations and evaluations.

Proper use of COLES NOTES will allow the student to pay greater attention to lectures and spend less time taking notes. This will result in a broader understanding of the work being studied and will free the student for increased participation in discussions.

COLES NOTES are an invaluable aid for review and exam preparation as well as an invitation to explore different interpretive paths.

COLES NOTES are written by experts in their fields. It should be noted that any literary judgement expressed herein is just that — the judgement of one school of thought. Interpretations that diverge from, or totally disagree with any criticism may be equally valid.

COLES NOTES are designed to supplement the text and are not intended as a substitute for reading the text itself. Use of the NOTES will serve not only to clarify the work being studied, but should enhance the reader's enjoyment of the topic.

ISBN 0-7740-3747-4

© COPYRIGHT 1996 AND PUBLISHED BY
COLES PUBLISHING COMPANY
TORONTO—CANADA
PRINTED IN CANADA

Manufactured by Webcom Limited
Cover finish: Webcom's Exclusive **Duracoat**

CONTENTS

Part A: The Play in Brief

Introduction

As enjoyable and important as Shakespeare's plays are, they can be difficult to read. Since Shakespeare wrote his plays to appeal to Elizabethan audiences, much of the text is dated and means little to the average reader of today.

We are, therefore, presenting the substance of the play in readable form by eliminating, as much as possible, the outdated passages and by paraphrasing the more complicated ones. This will give you a better understanding and appreciation of the play, and will make the questions and answers more meaningful.

CHARACTERS IN THE PLAY

Duncan: King of Scotland.

Malcolm
Donalbain } Duncan's sons.

Macbeth
Banquo } Generals.

Macduff
Lennox
Ross
Menteith } Scottish noblemen.
Angus
Caithness

Fleance: Banquo's son.

Siward: Earl of Northumberland; general of the English forces.

Young Siward: Siward's son.

Seyton: Macbeth's officer.

Boy: Macduff's son.

An English Doctor

A Scottish Doctor

A Sergeant

A Porter

An Old Man

Lady Macbeth

Lady Macduff

Hecate

Three Witches

Apparitions

Lords, Gentlemen, Gentlewomen, Officers, Soldiers and Attendants

[*Setting: Scotland and England.*]

1

ACT I

Practically all the action of this tragic masterpiece takes place in Scotland. The play opens on a deserted heath, where three withered witches in wild dress appear against a background of thunder and lightning. They begin to recite an eerie chant:

First Witch: When shall we three meet again
In thunder, lightning, or in rain?
Second Witch: When the hurlyburly's done,
When the battle's lost and won.
Third Witch: That will be ere the set of sun.
First Witch: Where the place?
Second Witch: Upon the heath.
Third Witch: There to meet with Macbeth.
First Witch: I come, Graymalkin.
All: Paddock calls: anon!
Fair is foul, and foul is fair.
Hover through the fog and filthy air.

The action of the next scene begins at the camp of Duncan, near Forres in Scotland, where a wounded sergeant is informing the king of the courageous deeds of two Scottish lords, Macbeth and Banquo, in battle against the king of Norway, who was aided by the thane of Cawdor, a traitorous Scot. Cawdor has been captured. Duncan orders that he be executed and that his title be conferred upon Macbeth because of his bravery.

It is now late on the same day. Again, the witches appear as thunder rolls. They tell each other what evil deeds they have been busy with. The first witch, out of vengeance against a sailor's wife, who would not give her the chestnuts she asked for, caused the winds to be unfavorable, so that the sailor had to remain at sea for 81 weeks without sleep.

Macbeth and Banquo enter. Macbeth's first words, "So fair and foul a day I have not seen," echo the earlier chant of the witches. The two lords are startled by the strange appearance of the witches. Banquo wonders:

What are these
So wither'd, and so wild in their attire,
That look not like the inhabitants o' the earth,
And yet are on 't? Live you? or are you aught

That man may question? You seem to understand me,
By each at once her choppy finger laying
Upon her skinny lips: you should be women,
And yet your beards forbid me to interpret
That you are so.

The witches greet Macbeth as the thane of Glamis, the thane
of Cawdor and the future king. Banquo asks Macbeth, "why do
you start and seem to fear/Things that do sound so fair?" The
witches then greet Banquo as one "Lesser than Macbeth, and
greater," "Not so happy, yet much happier." They also predict
that Banquo "shalt get kings, though . . . be none."

Macbeth asks these "imperfect speakers" to stay and tell
more, but the witches vanish. After their disappearance, Banquo
wonders:

Were such things here as we do speak about?
Or have we eaten on the insane root
That takes the reason prisoner?

Macbeth and Banquo discuss the witches' prophecies until
their talk is interrupted by Ross, who comes to announce that
Macbeth has been made thane of Cawdor. "What! can the Devil
speak true?" exclaims Banquo, while Macbeth remarks in an
aside:

Glamis, and thane of Cawdor:
The greatest is behind. Thanks for your pains.
Do you not hope your children shall be kings,
When those that gave the thane of Cawdor to me
Promised no less to them?

Banquo warns Macbeth that "oftentimes, to win us to our
harm,/The instruments of darkness tell us truths." Macbeth
disregards Banquo's warning and accepts these truths as "happy
prologues to the swelling act/Of the imperial theme." Macbeth's
aside continues:

This supernatural soliciting
Cannot be ill; cannot be good: if ill,
Why hath it given me earnest of success,
Commencing in a truth? I am thane of Cawdor:

If good, why do I yield to that suggestion
Whose horrid image doth unfix my hair
And make my seated heart knock at my ribs,
Against the use of nature? Present fears
Are less than horrible imaginings:
My thought, whose murder yet is but fantastical,
Shakes so my single state of man that function
Is smother'd in surmise, and nothing is
But what is not.
Banquo: Look, how our partner's rapt.
Macbeth: [*Aside*] If chance will have me king, why,
chance may crown me,
Without my stir.
Banquo: New honours come upon him,
Like our strange garments, cleave not to their mould
But with the aid of use.
Macbeth: [*Aside*] Come what come may,
Time and the hour runs through the roughest day.

Macbeth and Banquo return to the palace at Forres, where
Duncan has just been informed of Cawdor's execution. The king
comments:

There's no art
To find the mind's construction in the face:
He was a gentleman on whom I built
An absolute trust.

Macbeth and the others appear, and Duncan welcomes them
cordially:

More is thy due than more than all can pay.

Macbeth says that he has done no more than his duty, and Banquo agrees. Duncan announces that he is making Malcolm heir to
the throne. He further says that he is planning to stay that night
with Macbeth at Inverness. Macbeth goes ahead to prepare for
the visit, disturbed by the announcement regarding Malcolm:

The Prince of Cumberland! That is a step
On which I must fall down, or else o'erleap,

For in my way it lies. Stars, hide your fires;
Let not light see my black and deep desires:
The eye wink at the hand; yet let that be
Which the eye fears, when it is done, to see.

The scene changes to Macbeth's castle in Inverness. Macbeth has already sent his wife a letter describing the witches and telling of their prophecies, the first of which has come true: he is thane of Cawdor. He knows Lady Macbeth will rejoice with him. After she has read the letter, she says to herself:

Glamis thou art, and Cawdor, and shalt be
What thou art promised: yet do I fear thy nature;
It is too full o' the milk of human kindness
To catch the nearest way: thou wouldst be great;
Art not without ambition, but without
The illness should attend it: what thou wouldst
highly,
That wouldst thou holily; wouldst not play false,
And yet wouldst wrongly win: thou'ldst have, great
Glamis,
That which cries 'Thus thou must do, if thou have it;
And that which rather thou dost fear to do
Than wishest should be undone.' Hie thee hither,
That I may pour my spirits in thine ear,
And chastise with the valour of my tongue
All that impedes thee from the golden round,
Which fate and metaphysical aid doth seem
To have thee crown'd withal.

A messenger arrives to inform Lady Macbeth of Duncan's plans to visit Inverness that night. In a soliloquy, Lady Macbeth reveals her ambitions for her husband and her desire to carry out her plans without remorse:

The raven himself is hoarse
That croaks the fatal entrance of Duncan
Under my battlements. Come, you spirits
That tend on mortal thoughts, unsex me here,
And fill me, from the crown to the toe, top-full
Of direst cruelty! make thick my blood,

Stop up the access and passage to remorse,
That no compunctious visitings of nature
Shake my fell purpose, nor keep peace between
The effect and it! Come to my woman's breasts,
And take my milk for gall, you murdering ministers,
Wherever in your sightless substances
You wait on nature's mischief! Come, thick night,
And pall thee in the dunnest smoke of hell,
That my keen knife see not the wound it makes,
Nor heaven peep through the blanket of the dark,
To cry 'Hold, hold!'

When Macbeth enters, she greets him proudly as "Great Glamis! worthy Cawdor!/Greater than both, by the all-hail hereafter!" Noticing Macbeth's worried expression, she tells him:

Your face, my thane, is as a book where men
May read strange matters. To beguile the time,
Look like the time; bear welcome in your eye,
Your hand, your tongue: look like the innocent
flower,
But be the serpent under 't. He that's coming
Must be provided for: and you shall put
This night's great business into my dispatch;
Which shall to all our nights and days to come
Give solely sovereign sway and masterdom.

As Duncan and Banquo approach Macbeth's castle, Duncan remarks:

This castle hath a pleasant seat; the air
Nimbly and sweetly recommends itself
Unto our gentle senses.
Banquo: This guest of summer,
The temple-haunting martlet, does approve
By his loved mansionry that the heaven's breath
Smells wooingly here: no jutty, frieze,
Buttress, nor coign of vantage, but this bird
Hath made his pendent bed and procreant cradle:
Where they most breed and haunt, I have observed
The air is delicate.

Lady Macbeth enters and receives them with a great show of loyalty. In return, Duncan forecasts greater honors for her husband.

A short time later, while Duncan is being feasted in the castle, Macbeth, greatly troubled, leaves the banquet hall to consider the terrible deed he is about to commit:

If it were done when 'tis done, then 'twere well
It were done quickly: if the assassination
Could trammel up the consequence, and catch,
With his surcease, success; that but this blow
Might be the be-all and the end-all here,
But here, upon this bank and shoal of time,
We'ld jump the life to come. But in these cases
We still have judgement here; that we but teach
Bloody instructions, which being taught return
To plague the inventor: this even-handed justice
Commends the ingredients of our poison'd chalice
To our own lips. He's here in double trust:
First, as I am his kinsman and his subject,
Strong both against the deed; then, as his host,
Who should against his murderer shut the door,
Not bear the knife myself. Besides, this Duncan
Hath borne his faculties so meek, hath been
So clear in his great office, that his virtues
Will plead like angels trumpet-tongued against
The deep damnation of his taking-off;
And pity, like a naked new-born babe,
Striding the blast, or heaven's cherubin horsed
Upon the sightless couriers of the air,
Shall blow the horrid deed in every eye,
That tears shall drown the wind. I have no spur
To prick the sides of my intent, but only
Vaulting ambition, which o'erleaps itself
And falls on the other.

Lady Macbeth, worried by her husband's absence, enters and scolds him for having left the feast. When Macbeth tells her that they will not go through with the murder, she responds angrily:

Was the hope drunk
Wherein you dress'd yourself? hath it slept since?

And wakes it now, to look so green and pale
At what it did so freely?

She then accuses Macbeth of lacking manhood:

What beast was't then
That made you break this enterprise to me?
When you durst do it, then you were a man;
And, to be more than what you were, you would
Be so much more the man. Nor time nor place
Did then adhere, and yet you would make both:
They have made themselves, and that their fitness
now
Does unmake you. I have given suck, and know
How tender 'tis to love the babe that milks me:
I would, while it was smiling in my face,
Have pluck'd my nipple from his boneless gums,
And dash'd the brains out, had I so sworn as you
Have done to this.

Macbeth expresses fear that their plans will fail, but Lady
Macbeth assures him: "But screw your courage to the sticking
place,/And we'll not fail." Encouraged by her brave words,
Macbeth praises his wife:

Bring forth men-children only;
For thy undaunted mettle should compose
Nothing but males,

They complete their plans for the murder. They will use the
daggers of Duncan's two manservants to murder the sleeping
king. So that suspicion for the murder will not fall on Macbeth
and Lady Macbeth, the two agree to smear the servants with
blood and make their "griefs and clamour roar/Upon
[Duncan's] death." Now fully determined to commit the murder,
Macbeth exclaims:

I am settled, and bend up
Each corporal agent to this terrible feat.
Away, and mock the time with fairest show:
False face must hide what the false heart doth know.

ACT II

Late that same night, Banquo and Fleance are preparing to leave, when Macbeth appears. They tell him that the king has already gone to bed. Banquo happens to remark that he has dreamed of the weird sisters. Macbeth pretends that he has not thought of them, but he remarks that he would like to talk about them with Banquo another time. Macbeth speaks vaguely about Banquo's supporting him in the future and being rewarded for it. Banquo consents, provided that he will also be able to remain loyal to the king. Fleance and Banquo go, leaving Macbeth alone.

Macbeth waits for the sound of the bell, which is to be the signal that the preparations for the murder of Duncan have been completed. As he waits, he hallucinates:

Is this a dagger which I see before me,
The handle toward my hand? Come, let me clutch
thee.
I have thee not, and yet I see thee still.
Art thou not, fatal vision, sensible
To feeling as to sight? or art thou but
A dagger of the mind, a false creation,
Proceeding from the heat-oppressed brain?
I see thee yet, in form as palpable
As this which now I draw.
Thou marshall'st me the way that I was going;
And such an instrument I was to use.
Mine eyes are made the fools o' the other senses,
Or else worth all the rest: I see thee still;
And on thy blade and dudgeon gouts of blood,
Which was not so before. There's no such thing:
It is the bloody business which informs
Thus to mine eyes. Now o'er the one half-world
Nature seems dead, and wicked dreams abuse
The curtain'd sleep; witchcraft celebrates
Pale Hecate's offerings; and wither'd murder,
Alarum'd by his sentinel, the wolf,
Whose howl's his watch, thus with his stealthy pace,
With Tarquin's ravishing strides, towards his design
Moves like a ghost. Thou sure and firm-set earth,
Hear not my steps, which way they walk, for fear

Thy very stones prate of my whereabout,
And take the present horror from the time,
Which now suits with it. Whiles I threat, he lives:
Words to the heat of deeds too cold breath gives.

[*A bell rings*]

I go, and it is done: the bell invites me.
Hear it not, Duncan, for it is a knell
That summons thee to heaven, or to hell.

When he is gone, Lady Macbeth comes from the room where
Duncan is sleeping:

That which hath made them drunk hath made me
bold;
What hath quench'd them hath given me fire. Hark!
Peace!
It was the owl that shriek'd, the fatal bellman,
Which gives the stern'st good-night. He is about it:
The doors are open, and the surfeited grooms
Do mock their charge with snores: I have drugg'd
their possets,
That death and nature do contend about them,
Whether they live or die.

Lady Macbeth imagines her husband murdering Duncan and
remarks that she would have killed the king herself "Had he not
resembled/My father as he slept." Hearing a cry, Lady Macbeth
wonders if all is going according to plan. A few moments later,
Macbeth enters and describes what happened.

After having committed the murder, Macbeth passed a room
in which a man called out "Murder!" in his sleep, waking his
companion. The two men were Donalbain, the king's son, and
his attendant. One of them cried, "God bless us!" but Macbeth
was unable to give the automatic reply to a blessing, for the word,
amen, stuck in his throat. Macbeth imagined he heard a voice cry
"Sleep no more!/Macbeth does murder sleep." The voice continued to torment Macbeth by proclaiming that, since "Glamis
hath murdered sleep, . . . Cawdor/Shall sleep no more."

Lady Macbeth urges her husband to come to his senses:

Who was it that thus cried? Why, worthy thane,
You do unbend your noble strength, to think

So brainsickly of things. Go get some water,
And wash this filthy witness from your hand.
Why did you bring these daggers from the place?
They must lie there: go carry them, and smear
The sleepy grooms with blood.
Macbeth: I'll go no more:
I am afraid to think what I have done;
Look on 't again I dare not.
Lady Macbeth: Infirm of purpose!
Give me the daggers: the sleeping and the dead
Are but as pictures: 'tis the eye of childhood
That fears a painted devil. If he do bleed,
I'll gild the faces of the grooms withal,
For it must seem their guilt.

A sudden knocking at the gate startles Macbeth, who wishes that the sound could waken Duncan. Lady Macbeth hurries her husband off to wash his hands and change into his dressing gown.

A drunken porter goes to answer the knocking at the gate. It occurs to him that the porter at the gates of hell must be even busier than he is. He then pretends that he is the porter at hell-gate and that he is admitting various sinners.

The porter finally opens the gate, and Macduff and Lennox, two of the king's noblemen, enter. Macbeth appears in his dressing gown to meet them. While Macbeth talks to Lennox, Macduff goes to wake the king. Lennox remarks on the strange disturbance in nature during the night: chimneys were blown down, the earth seemed to shake and owl-screechings and eerie screams were heard. "'Twas a rough night," replies Macbeth simply.

Macduff returns, crying out in horror. Macbeth and Lennox rush to Duncan's chamber, while Macduff orders that the alarm be rung. Lady Macbeth, Banquo, Malcolm and Donalbain enter hurriedly, and Macbeth and Lennox return. Macbeth remarks:

Had I but died an hour before this chance,
I had lived a blessed time; for from this instant
There's nothing serious in mortality:
All is but toys: renown and grace is dead;
The wine of life is drawn, and the mere lees
Is left this vault to brag of.

Lennox offers the apparent explanation for Duncan's death:

Those of his chamber, as it seem'd, had done 't:
Their hands and faces were all badged with blood;
So were their daggers, which unwiped we found
Upon their pillows:
They stared, and were distracted; no man's life
Was to be trusted with them.

Macbeth, who has killed the servants, says that he wishes he hadn't done so, but:

The expedition of my violent love
Outrun the pauser, reason.

Lady Macbeth faints, and Banquo shouts:

Look to the lady:

[*Lady Macbeth is carried out*]
And when we have our naked frailties hid,
That suffer in exposure, let us meet,
And question this most bloody piece of work,
To know it further. Fears and scruples shake us:
In the great hand of God I stand, and thence
Against the undivulged pretence I fight
Of treasonous malice.

Macbeth suggests that they all "put on manly readiness, / And meet in the hall together."

Malcolm and Donalbain remain after the others leave. They express their fear and suspicion of their kinsmen and decide to escape while they can. Malcolm will go to England, Donalbain to Ireland.

It has been a disturbing night. Ross and an old man talk over the strange events: how a falcon was attacked by an owl and Duncan's horses went wild in their stables. Now Macduff enters and tells them that it is rumored that the king was murdered by his two sons, who have fled. He also brings news that Macbeth has gone to Scone to be made king. Scone is where Ross himself is going, but Macduff is going to skip the coronation and go home to Fife.

ACT III

Banquo has, by this time, become suspicious. He says of Macbeth:

Thou hast it now: king, Cawdor, Glamis, all,
As the weird women promised, and I fear
Thou play'dst most foully for 't: yet it was said
It should not stand in thy posterity,
But that myself should be the root and father
Of many kings. If there come truth from them —
As upon thee, Macbeth, their speeches shine —
Why, by the verities on thee made good,
May they not be my oracles as well
And set me up in hope? But hush, no more.

Macbeth and his queen come in with attendants, and
Macbeth, seeing Banquo, invites him to the banquet to be held
that evening. He makes sure that Banquo will return in time, for
he is riding away that afternoon with Fleance, who will return
with his father. As Banquo leaves, Macbeth dismisses the others,
saying that he will remain alone until supper.

He then summons two men who are waiting outside the
palace gate. While waiting for them to arrive, he expresses, in a
soliloquy, his fear of Banquo:

To be thus is nothing;
But to be safely thus: our fears in Banquo
Stick deep; and in his royalty of nature
Reigns that which would be fear'd: 'tis much he
dares,
And, to that dauntless temper of his mind,
He hath a wisdom that doth guide his valour
To act in safety. There is none but he
Whose being I do fear: and under him
My Genius is rebuked, as it is said
Mark Antony's was by Caesar. He chid the sisters,
When first they put the name of king upon me,
And bade them speak to him; then prophet-like
They hail'd him father to a line of kings:
Upon my head they placed a fruitless crown
And put a barren sceptre in my gripe,

Thence to be wrench'd with an unlineal hand,
No son of mine succeeding. If 't be so,
For Banquo's issue have I filed my mind;
For them the gracious Duncan have I murder'd;
Put rancours in the vessel of my peace
Only for them, and mine eternal jewel
Given to the common enemy of man,
To make them kings, the seed of Banquo kings!
Rather than so, come, fate, into the list,
And champion me to the utterance!

The men Macbeth has been waiting for, two murderers,
enter. Macbeth reminds them of an earlier conversation in which
he explained how Banquo is responsible for the unrest in the
kingdom. He then tells the men how they can avenge themselves
against Banquo and gain the favor of the throne if they murder
both Banquo and Fleance while the two are on the road. Macbeth
reminds the murderers to "leave no rubs nor botches in the
work."

It is now almost time for the banquet. Lady Macbeth comes
into the room and sends a servant to find the king. She is evidently anxious:

Nought's had, all's spent,
Where our desire is got without content:
'Tis safer to be that which we destroy
Than by destruction dwell in doubtful joy.

Macbeth enters, and the conversation between him and Lady
Macbeth reveals a change in their relationship. Macbeth shows
new strength and independence as he reveals how he is prepared
to stop at nothing to fulfil his ambitions:

We have scotch'd the snake, not kill'd it:
She'll close and be herself, whilst our poor malice
Remains in danger of her former tooth.
But let the frame of things disjoint, both the worlds
suffer
Ere we will eat our meal in fear, and sleep
In the affliction of these terrible dreams
That shake us nightly: better be with the dead,

Whom we, to gain our peace, have sent to peace,
Than on the torture of the mind to lie
In restless ecstasy. Duncan is in his grave;
After life's fitful fever he sleeps well;
Treason has done his worst: nor steel, nor poison,
Malice domestic, foreign levy, nothing,
Can touch him further.

Lady Macbeth: Come on;
Gentle my lord, sleek o'er your rugged looks;
Be bright and jovial among your guests to-night.

Macbeth: So shall I, love; and so, I pray, be you:
Let your remembrance apply to Banquo;
Present him eminence, both with eye and tongue:
Unsafe the while, that we
Must lave our honours in these flattering streams,
And make our faces visards to our hearts,
Disguising what they are.

Lady Macbeth: You must leave this.

Macbeth: O, full of scorpions is my mind, dear wife!
Thou know'st that Banquo, and his Fleance, lives.

Lady Macbeth: But in them nature's copy's not
enterne.

Macbeth: There's comfort yet; they are assailable;
Then be thou jocund: ere the bat hath flown
His cloister'd flight; ere to black Hecate's summons
The shard-borne beetle with his drowsy hums
Hath rung night's yawning peal, there shall be done
A deed of dreadful note.

Lady Macbeth: What's to be done?

Macbeth: Be innocent of the knowledge, dearest
chuck,
Till thou applaud the deed. Come, seeling night,
Scarf up the tender eye of pitiful day,
And with thy bloody and invisible hand
Cancel and tear to pieces that great bond
Which keeps me pale! Light thickens, and the crow
Makes wing to the rooky wood:
Good things of day being to droop and drowse,
Whiles night's black agents to their preys do rouse.
Thou marvell'st at my words: but hold thee still;
Things bad begun make strong themselves by ill:
So, prithee, go with me.

In the castle park, three murderers await the return of Banquo and Fleance. As they appear with a torch, the murderers ambush them and kill Banquo, but Fleance escapes. The murderers then go to report to the king, who is greeting his guests. Macbeth leaves the festivities for a moment to speak to the first murderer at the door. He is delighted to hear that Banquo is dead, but he is greatly disturbed to learn of Fleance's escape. Macbeth returns to his guests and expresses his regret at the absence of Banquo.

Macbeth suddenly notices the ghost of Banquo seated in his own place at the head of the table. Macbeth addresses the spirit wildly:

> Thou canst not say I did it: never shake
> Thy gory locks at me.

Lady Macbeth attempts to reassure the guests that Macbeth's "fit is momentary." Then, she turns to Macbeth and ask scornfully, "Are you a man?" She berates her husband for his weakness of mind:

> O proper stuff!
> This is the very painting of your fear:
> This is the air-drawn dagger which, you said,
> Led you to Duncan. O, these flaws and starts,
> Impostors to true fear, would well become
> A woman's story at a winter's fire,
> Authorized by her grandam. Shame itself!
> Why do you make such faces? When all's done,
> You look but on a stool.

Lady Macbeth concludes that her husband is "quite unmann'd in folly." She reminds him about his obligations as a host, and Macbeth recovers himself enough to explain that he has "a strange infirmity, which is nothing," and to encourage his guests to drink and be merry. The ghost reappears, though, and Macbeth is once more shaken:

> Avaunt! and quit my sight! let the earth hide thee!
> Thy bones are marrowless, thy blood is cold;
> Thou hast no speculation in those eyes
> Which thou dost glare with.

16

Regaining his composure, Macbeth again urges that the festivities continue, but Lady Macbeth remarks:

You have displaced the mirth, broke the good
meeting,
With most admired disorder.

The party breaks up, and Macbeth, alone with his wife, expresses his horror at what he has witnessed. Then, he turns to more practical considerations: the possible threat posed by Macduff, who did not attend the feast. Macbeth states his intention to visit the witches:

I will to-morrow,
And betimes I will, to the weird sisters:
More shall they speak, for now I am bent to know,
By the worst means, the worst. For mine own good
All causes shall give way: I am in blood
Stepp'd in so far that, should I wade no more,
Returning were as tedious as go o'er:
Strange things I have in head that will to hand,
Which must be acted ere they may be scann'd.

"You lack the season of all natures, sleep," Lady Macbeth tells her agitated husband, who replies:

Come, we'll to sleep. My strange and self-abuse
Is the initiate fear that wants hard use:
We are yet but young in deed.

Again, the three witches appear upon the heath, where they meet with a fourth, Hecate, their queen, who orders them to appear with her in the morning at a spot where Macbeth is coming to learn his fate. Hecate plans to raise false visions that will deceive Macbeth.

Lennox and another lord are in the palace discussing how Macbeth killed the two grooms and how he would punish Duncan's sons if they had a chance. Malcolm, who had fled to England, has obtained the support of the English king in his plans to overthrow Macbeth. War is the immediate prospect.

ACT IV

The next morning in a dark cave, the witches gather around a boiling cauldron:

First Witch: Round about the cauldron go:
In the poison'd entrails throw.
Toad, that under cold stone
Days and nights has thirty one
Swelter'd venom sleeping got,
Boil thou first i' the charmed pot.
All: Double, double toil and trouble;
Fire burn and cauldron bubble.
Second Witch: Fillet of a fenny snake,
In the cauldron boil and bake;
Eye of newt and toe of frog,
Wool of bat and tongue of dog,
Adder's fork and blind-worm's sting,
Lizard's leg and howlet's wing,
For a charm of powerful trouble,
Like a hell-broth boil and bubble.
All: Double, double toil and trouble;
Fire burn and cauldron bubble.
Third Witch: Scale of dragon, tooth of wolf,
Witches' mummy, maw and gulf
Of the ravin'd salt-sea shark,
Root of hemlock digg'd i' the dark,
Liver of blaspheming Jew,
Gall of goat and slips of yew
Sliver'd in the moon's eclipse,
Nose of Turk and Tartar's lips,
Finger of birth-strangled babe
Ditch-deliver'd by a drab,
Make the gruel thick and slab:
Add thereto a tiger's chaudron,
For the ingredients of our cauldron.
All: Double, double toil and trouble;
Fire burn and cauldron bubble.
Second Witch: Cool it with a baboon's blood,
Then the charm is firm and good.

Macbeth approaches and greets the "secret, black, and midnight hags." He demands to know the answers to his questions. The witches produce an apparition, a head in armor that anticipates Macbeth's questions and tells him to beware of Macduff. Then, they produce a second apparition, a bloody child, which tells Macbeth that no man born of woman can harm him. The third apparition, a child, crowned, with a tree in his hand, tells him that he shall never be defeated until "Great Birnam Wood to high Dunsinane hill/Shall come against him."

Macbeth, pleased with these predictions, asks whether Banquo's heirs will ever rule in this kingdom. He is shown a procession of eight kings, the last carrying a mirror, and Banquo's bloody ghost following. In the eighth king's mirror, Macbeth sees many more kings, whom Banquo points out as his. The witches mockingly dance around and vanish.

Macbeth, now very upset, calls to Lennox, who has been standing guard outside the cave. Lennox tells Macbeth that he has just learned from several messengers that Macduff has escaped to England.

Macbeth, in an aside, reveals his plan to have Lady Macduff and her children murdered:

Time, thou anticipatest my dread exploits:
The flighty purpose never is o'ertook
Unless the deed go with it: from this moment
The very firstlings of my heart shall be
The firstlings of my hand. And even now,
To crown my thoughts with acts, be it thought and done:
The castle of Macduff I will surprise;
Seize upon Fife; give to the edge o' the sword
His wife, his babes, and all unfortunate souls
That trace him in his line. No boasting like a fool;
This deed I'll do before this purpose cool:
But no more sights!

In Macduff's castle in Fife, Lady Macduff complains to Ross about her husband's escape to England:

Wisdom! to leave his wife, to leave his babes,
His mansion and his titles, in a place
From whence himself does fly? He loves us not;

He wants the natural touch: for the poor wren,
The most diminutive of birds, will fight,
Her young ones in her nest, against the owl.
All is the fear and nothing is the love;
As little is the wisdom, where the flight
So runs against all reason.

Ross attempts to justify Macduff's actions:

My dearest coz,
I pray you, school yourself: but, for your husband,
He is noble, wise, judicious, and best knows
The fits o' the season. I dare not speak much further:
But cruel are the times, when we are traitors
And do not know ourselves; when we hold rumour
From what we fear, yet know not what we fear,
But float upon a wild and violent sea
Each way and move. I take my leave of you:
Shall not be long but I'll be here again:
Things at the worst will cease, or else climb upward
To what they were before.

After Ross leaves, Lady Macduff and her son continue talk-ing about his father and his reasons for leaving them. They are in-terrupted by a messenger, who warns them to flee at once because they are in desperate danger. Lady Macduff says:

Whither should I fly?
I have done no harm. But I remember now
I am in this earthly world, where to do harm
Is often laudable, to do good sometime
Accounted dangerous folly: why then, alas,
Do I put up that womanly defence,
To say I have done no harm?

The murderers sent by Macbeth burst in and kill them both.
Macduff has, in the meantime, reached England, where he is talking with Malcolm. They both regret Scotland's sad fate, but Malcolm distrusts Macduff. Many agents of Macbeth have ap-proached him, and Macduff may be another:

Angels are bright still, though the brightest fell.

Malcolm now gives Macduff a summary of his own sins, far worse than those of Macbeth. He ends by saying:

> The king-becoming graces,
> As justice, verity, temperance, stableness,
> Bounty, perseverance, mercy, lowliness,
> Devotion, patience, courage, fortitude,
> I have no relish of them, but abound
> In the division of each several crime,
> Acting in many ways. Nay, had I power, I should
> Pour the sweet milk of concord into hell,
> Uproar the universal peace, confound
> All unity on earth.

Hearing this, Macduff is overwhelmed and gives up hope of any salvation for his country. But then Malcolm, convinced of Macduff's evident sincerity, denies the evil he has spoken of himself. He reassures Macduff of his loyalty to Scotland.

Ross now brings news from Scotland. Macduff welcomes him and asks:

> Stands Scotland where it did?
> **Ross:** Alas, poor country!
> Almost afraid to know itself! It cannot
> Be call'd our mother, but our grave: where nothing,
> But who knows nothing, is once seen to smile;
> Where sighs and groans and shrieks that rend the air,
> Are made, not mark'd; where violent sorrow seems
> A modern ecstasy: the dead man's knell
> Is there scarce ask'd for who; and good men's lives
> Expire before the flowers in their caps,
> Dying or ere they sicken.

Ross then assures Macduff that his wife and family "were well at peace when I did leave them," but he finally reveals the truth:

> Your castle is surprised; your wife and babes
> Savagely slaughter'd: to relate the manner,
> Were, on the quarry of these murder'd deer,
> To add the death of you.

Macduff's response is one of astonishment and gentle pity for his family:

All my pretty ones?
Did you say all? O hell-kite! All?
What, all my pretty chickens and their dam
At one fell swoop?

Malcolm advises Macduff to "Dispute it like a man." He adds:

Be this the whetstone of your sword: let grief
Convert to anger, blunt not the heart, enrage it.

Macduff's grief becomes more "manly" gradually:

O, I could play the woman with mine eyes,
And braggart with my tongue! But, gentle heavens,
Cut short all intermission; front to front
Bring thou this fiend of Scotland and myself;
Within my word's length set him; if he 'scape,
Heaven forgive him too!

ACT V

It is night, and, in the castle at Dunsinane, Lady Macbeth's gentlewoman is describing to a doctor how her mistress has been walking in her sleep recently. Lady Macbeth enters, carrying a candle. Although her eyes are open, "their sense is shut." Lady Macbeth begins to speak, reliving the nights that Duncan and Banquo were murdered and trying desperately to clean the imaginary blood off her hands:

> Out, damned spot! out, I say! One: two: why, then 'tis time to do 't. Hell is murky. Fie, my lord, fie! a soldier, and afeard? What need we fear who knows it, when none can call our power to account? Yet who would have thought the old man to have had so much blood in him?

When she thinks her hands are finally clean, she examines them more closely and finds:

> Here's the smell of the blood still: all the perfumes of Arabia will not sweeten this little hand. Oh, oh, oh!

The gentlewoman and doctor listen in horror as Lady Macbeth reveals the dark secrets that lie behind her guilty behavior. The doctor comments that her "disease" cannot be cured by him. He goes on to observe:

> Foul whisperings are abroad: unnatural deeds
> Do breed unnatural troubles: infected minds
> To their deaf pillows will discharge their secrets:
> More needs she the divine than the physician.
> God, God forgive us all! Look after her;
> Remove from her the means of all annoyance,
> And still keep eyes upon her. So good night:
> My mind she has mated and amazed my sight:
> I think, but dare not speak.

A group of Scots is marching to meet the forces of Malcolm and old Siward at Birnam Wood. They hear that the king is very upset because he realizes that his subjects hate him.

Macbeth's feelings are revealed as he talks with a doctor and with his servants during the battle:

Bring me no more reports; let them fly all:
Till Birnam Wood remove to Dunsinane
I cannot taint with fear. What's the boy Malcolm?
Was he not born of woman? The spirits that know
All mortal consequences have pronounced me thus:
'Fear not, Macbeth; no man that's born of woman
Shall e'er have power upon thee.' Then fly, false
thanes,
And mingle with the English epicures:
The mind I sway by and the heart I bear
Shall never sag with doubt nor shake with fear.

The doctor tells Macbeth that Lady Macbeth is not physical-
ly ill, but deeply troubled mentally. Macbeth replies impatiently:

Cure her of that.
Canst thou not minister to a mind diseased,
Pluck from the memory a rooted sorrow,
Raze out the written troubles of the brain,
And with some sweet oblivious antidote
Cleanse the stuff'd bosom of that perilous stuff
Which weighs upon the heart?

"Therein the patient/Must minister to himself," replies the
doctor. Speaking confusedly about his wife's illness, then about
the illness of Scotland, Macbeth prepares for battle:

Throw physic to the dogs, I'll none of it.
Come, put mine armour on; give me my staff.
Seyton, send out. Doctor, the thanes fly from me.
Come, sir, dispatch. It thou couldst, doctor, cast
The water of my land, find her disease
And purge it to a sound and pristine health,
I would applaud thee to the very echo,
That should applaud again. Pull 't off, I say.
What rhubarb, senna, or what purgative drug,
Would scour these English hence? Hear'st thou of
them?

As the English forces and their Scottish allies march through
Birnam Wood, Malcolm orders each soldier to carry in front of
him a branch cut from the wood in order to conceal their

numbers. Thus camouflaged, they continue their march toward
Dunsinane, where Macbeth is ordering his defence:

> Hang out our banners on the outward walls;
> The cry is still 'They come': our castle's strength
> Will laugh a siege to scorn: here let them lie
> Till famine and the ague eat them up:
> Were they not forced with those that should be ours,
> We might have met them dareful, beard to beard,
> And beat them backward home.

Just then, the cries of women are heard. Macbeth does not
recognize the sound until Seyton identifies it. Macbeth comments:

> I have almost forgot the taste of fears:
> The time has been, my senses would have cool'd
> To hear a night-shriek, and my fell of hair
> Would at a dismal treatise rouse and stir
> As life were in 't: I have supp'd full with horrors;
> Direness, familiar to my slaughterous thoughts,
> Cannot once start me.

Seyton, who has gone to find out the reason for the cries,
returns and announces the death of Lady Macbeth. Macbeth's
response is unemotional, but grim:

> She should have died hereafter;
> There would have been a time for such a word.
> To-morrow, and to-morrow, and to-morrow,
> Creeps in this petty pace from day to day,
> To the last syllable of recorded time;
> And all our yesterdays have lighted fools
> The way to dusty death. Out, out, brief candle!
> Life's but a walking shadow, a poor player
> That struts and frets his hour upon the stage
> And then is heard no more: it is a tale
> Told by an idiot, full of sound and fury,
> Signifying nothing.

A messenger enters with the surprising news that Birnam
Wood has begun to move. Macbeth is stunned by this announcement:

I pull in resolution, and begin
To doubt the equivocation of the fiend
That lies like truth: 'Fear not, till Birnam Wood
Do come to Dunsinane'; and now a wood
Comes toward Dunsinane. Arm, arm, and out!
If this which he avouches does appear,
There is nor flying hence nor tarrying here.
I 'gin to be a-weary of the sun,
And wish the estate o' the world were now undone.
Ring the alarum-bell! Blow, wind! come, wrack!
At least we'll die with harness on our back.

Malcolm's forces march toward the castle and throw down
their branches in order to join battle. Macbeth appears, exclaim-
ing:

They have tied me to a stake; I cannot fly,
But bear-like I must fight the course. What's he
That was not born of woman? Such a one
Am I to fear, or none.

He is met by young Siward, who bravely fights him and
whom he kills. Macbeth then rushes away, shouting:

Thou wast born of woman.
But swords I smile at, weapons laugh to scorn,
Brandish'd by man that's of a woman born.

But Macduff now comes searching for the murderer of his
family. He says:

That way the noise is. Tyrant, show thy face!
If thou be'st slain and with no stroke of mine,
My wife and children's ghosts will haunt me still.
I cannot strike at wretched kerns, whose arms
Are hired to bear their staves: either thou, Macbeth,
Or else my sword, with an unbatter'd edge,
I sheathe again undeeded. There thou shouldst be;
By this great clatter, one of greatest note
Seems bruited: let me find him, fortune!
And more I beg not.

Meanwhile, the castle is surrounded, and Macbeth comes back again, saying:

Why should I play the Roman fool, and die
On mine own sword? whiles I see lives, the gashes
Do better upon them.

Macduff enters and challenges Macbeth, who confidently assures Macduff that all efforts to defeat him are useless:

Let fall thy blade on vulnerable crests;
I bear a charmed life, which must not yield
To one of woman born.

But Macbeth receives another surprise when Macduff informs him:

Despair thy charm,
And let the angel whom thou still hast served
Tell thee, Macduff was from his mother's womb
Untimely ripp'd.

Macbeth's initial response to Macduff's words is a refusal to fight:

Accursed be that tongue that tells me so,
For it hath cow'd my better part of man!
And be these juggling fiends no more believed,
That palter with us in a double sense;
That keep the word of promise to our ear,
And break it to our hope. I'll not fight with thee.

On being told, however, that he will be made a captive to be exhibited to the people as a monster, Macbeth decides he "will try to the last."

In the castle, Malcolm expresses concern over the absence of Macduff and young Siward. Ross enters and informs Siward of his son's honorable death. Macduff enters, carrying Macbeth's head, mounted on a pole. Macduff addresses Malcolm:

Hail, king! for so thou art: behold, where stands

The usurper's cursed head: the time is free:
I see thee compass'd with thy kingdom's pearl,
That speak my salutation in their minds;
Whose voices I desire aloud with mine:
Hail, King of Scotland!

Malcolm accepts the kingship and closes the play with a
noble speech:

We shall not spend a large expense of time
Before we reckon with your several loves,
And make us even with you. My thanes and kinsmen,
Henceforth be earls, the first that ever Scotland
In such an honour named. What's more to do,
Which would be planted newly with the time,
As calling home our exiled friends abroad
That fled the snares of watchful tyranny,
Producing forth the cruel ministers
Of this dead butcher and his fiend-like queen,
Who, as 'tis thought, by self and violent hands
Took off her life; this, and what needful else
That calls upon us, by the grace of Grace
We will perform in measure, time and place:
So thanks to all at once and to each one,
Whom we invite to see us crown'd at Scone.

Part B: Questions and Answers by Act and Scene

ACT I • SCENE 1

Question 1.

How do the setting and atmosphere make the opening scene striking?

Answer

The opening scene of *Macbeth* is set in a deserted place, traditionally known as the "blasted heath." The wild, barren setting and the mysterious atmosphere created by thunder and lightning would intensify the horrifying physical appearance of the witches. The weird chanting and rhythmic speech (incantation) of the witches add to this atmosphere of horror and strangeness. This introductory scene, therefore, is striking in that it reinforces and contributes to the grim horror and terrible mystery that characterize the rest of the tragedy.

Question 2.

What information is given the audience through the conversation of the witches?

Answer

The audience learns, first, that the witches intend to meet Macbeth and, second, that they mean to do him harm. Then, we are told that a battle being fought will soon be won by Macbeth. We also learn that the witches can predict the future and that their familiars (attendant spirits) are present, in the form of a cat, a toad and an unknown — possibly Hecate. We gather that they are "instruments of darkness," or supernatural beings, who are both evil and spiteful in their words and actions.

Question 3.

What is the effect of the use of rhyme and so many strongly stressed syllables in the witches' speeches?

Answer

By prolonging the *-ain* rhyme, Shakespeare achieved a remarkably unpleasant whining effect. The three witches are distinguished from one another by different rhyme sounds. Thus, the first witch by *again + rain,* the second by *done + won,* while the third's *sun* echoes and continues the rhyme of the previous witch.

The climax of their chant comes with the rhymed couplet:

Fair is foul, and foul is fair
Hover through the fog and filthy air.

The use of several strongly stressed syllables adds force and direction to the words of the witches. They are to be feared; they are not weaklings, but powerful supernatural beings.

Question 4.
What is the meaning of the names, Graymalkin and Paddock? Explain the significance of their introduction into this scene.

Answer
Graymalkin, or Grimalkin, means a grey cat. Paddock, from the Anglo-Saxon word, pada, means toad. Cats and toads were forms commonly supposed to be assumed by witches and their familiar spirits. The witches themselves were, to some degree, subject to the influence of their attendant spirits. In this scene, which may be supposed to represent the end of a "witches' sabbath," the familiars appear to be calling away the witches for the purpose of instructing them in the duties that they will have to perform soon.

ACT I • SCENE 2
Question 1.
According to the conversation in Scene 2, what is the political condition of Scotland during the time *Macbeth* takes place?

Answer
Scotland lacks strong, decisive leadership. We may assume that King Duncan is a weak ruler because of the treachery of the thane of Cawdor and of Macdonwald. Scotland is faced with foreign invasion from Norway. In this dangerous political situation, one strong man stands out — Macbeth. He is recognized

for his bravery in battle (see the wounded sergeant's statement) and for his strong leadership. We learn later that the Norwegian king has been forced to make humiliating terms with the victorious Scots and that Cawdor has been captured. Duncan tells Ross to announce the order for Cawdor's immediate execution; the thaneship is to be transferred to Macbeth.

Question 2.

"A person's character is revealed in a play by what he does, by what he says, by what others say of him." According to Scene 2, what has Macbeth done to identify himself as the most commanding figure in Scotland? What are the tributes paid to Macbeth by Duncan, the soldier and Ross?

Answer

Macbeth has identified himself as the most commanding figure in Scotland by defeating the rebel army and by killing its leader, Macdonwald, in single combat. He has defeated the Norwegian king, Sweno, thus ending the threat of a foreign takeover. His courage, ability and active leadership distinguish him from the gentle, passive Duncan. Duncan praises him by referring to Macbeth as "valiant cousin! worthy gentleman!" The soldier calls him "brave Macbeth." Ross pays Macbeth tribute by naming him "Bellona's bridegroom."

Question 3.

What traits of Duncan's character are revealed in this scene?

Answer

Duncan is obviously good and gentle, but he lacks the strength needed in such troubled times to save Scotland from foreign invasion and internal treachery. He is generous in awarding credit where it is due, as is illustrated by his treatment of Macbeth after hearing of the victory. He seems to be passive, civilized and kind-hearted.

ACT I • SCENE 3

Question 1.

What powers were witches thought to possess in Shakespeare's time? What dramatic purpose is served by the revelation of these powers at this point in the play?

Answer

The power of casting an evil spell on pigs ("killing swine") was believed to be a common practice of witches during Elizabethan times and earlier. Witches were also thought to be able to sail the seas in sieves (just as they were often pictured flying broomsticks through the air). A cat without a tail was thought to be a witch that had taken the form of an animal. Witches were thought to have control over the winds. However, even the power of witches was limited, and some witches (such as Hecate) were thought to be more powerful than others. The textbook of the day on witchcraft was *Malleus Maleficarum* or *The Hammer of Witches* (1484). Shakespeare probably knew of, and may even have read, this book.

The dramatic purpose of these revelations is to suggest that these creatures possess powers that will prove difficult for Macbeth to overcome, if he attempts to resist them.

Question 2.

Discuss how the action of the plot thickens noticeably in this scene.

Answer

Macbeth and the witches are brought together in Scene 3. The witches make their predictions. Then, after having been informed by Ross that he has been made thane of Cawdor (one of the predictions has thus come true), Macbeth begins to trust the witches. He considers taking over the kingship and even thinks of murdering to achieve his ambitions. This scene thus speeds the central action of the plot.

Question 3.

Why are the predictions of the witches so quickly followed by the arrival of Ross and his news that Macbeth has been made thane of Cawdor?

Answer

The tempo (speed of action) of this drama is rapid. It is probable that Macbeth has toyed with the idea of one day becoming king. It is, therefore, good drama to have Ross and Angus arrive with the news of Macbeth's promotion, since it confirms the first of the predictions relating to Macbeth. If the first comes true, the second may also.

Question 4.
Before the appearance of the witches, had Macbeth thought about being king?

Answer
His shock, his "rapt" behavior, his eagerness for further information and his persistent references to the theme all point to the conclusion that the prophecy of the witches confirmed Macbeth's previous hopes. Perhaps the predictions also strengthened criminal intentions that he probably had never yet dared to express clearly, even to himself.

Question 5.
How are Macbeth and Banquo differently affected by the prophecies of the witches?

Answer
Macbeth is thrilled by the predictions and begins to think of becoming king. Banquo, on the contrary, recognizes the evil in the witches' prophecies. Whereas Macbeth seriously considers "the imperial theme," Banquo warns him that:

the instruments of darkness tell us truths,
Win us with honest trifles to betray us
In deepest consequences.

Question 6.
Distinguish between an aside and a soliloquy. What do you learn of Macbeth's character from his asides in Scene 3?

Answer
For the soliloquy, the character is alone on the stage, revealing his inner thoughts by speaking aloud. Thus, it is an artificial device that modern playwrights rarely employ. The aside is just as artificial, but it is more common. It consists of a character's turning away from the other characters on the stage, for the sake of addressing the audience privately, or just to think aloud. According to this convention, the other characters are unaware of what

is being said in the aside, though it must be impossible for them not to overhear what is being said.

Macbeth's asides in this scene reveal his innermost thoughts, which he must naturally conceal from Banquo and the others since they have to do with his ambition to become king. We have heard Macbeth being praised by others for his bravery as a soldier. Now we are given a chance to overhear Macbeth's view of himself and his hopes for the future.

ACT I • SCENE 4

Question 1.

For purposes of plot development, which are the two most important speeches in Scene 4?

Answer

From the point of view of the development of the plot, the two most important speeches would be those in which Duncan proclaims his son, Malcolm, heir to the throne and the one in which Macbeth (as a result of that announcement) once again considers murder in order to overcome this obstacle to his being crowned king. In Act I, Scene 3, 143, he expresses the hope that "chance," not action, would place him on the throne. Thus, the first speech is important as part of the complication, since it forces Macbeth to take action and leads to the rising action of the plot.

Question 2.

Define dramatic irony. Point out the irony of Duncan's speech in Act I, Scene 4, 11 to 14.

Answer

In dramatic irony, a double meaning is present in a speech, with the second meaning being obvious to the audience and often to the speaker or the characters on the stage. Usually, it is the speaker who is "in on the secret" with the audience, while the other characters are on the "outside."

In Act I, Scene 4, 11-14, the dramatic irony lies in the fact that the audience is aware that Duncan lacks the "art" of reading a person's character in his face. He greets Macbeth as his "worthiest cousin," but the audience knows that Macbeth has been planning to murder Duncan.

34

Question 3.

Macbeth feels goodness is desirable and should be practised, except when evil is necessary to achieve his ends. Discuss this view of Macbeth.

Answer

Macbeth declares, in his greeting to King Duncan, that:

The service and the loyalty I owe,
In doing it, pays itself. Your highness' part
Is to receive our duties: and our duties
Are to your throne and state, children and servants;
Which do but what they should, by doing everything
Safe toward your love and honour.

This speech shows that Macbeth is very much aware of his obligations to his king.

Later, after Malcolm has been made heir to the throne, Macbeth realizes that he has to overcome this obstacle somehow. He says, in an aside;

Stars, hide your fires,
Let not light see my black and deep desires:
The eye wink at the hand! yet let that be,
Which the eye fears, when it is done, to see.

The concept of the eye winking at the hand, or conscience ignoring one's actions, is basically immoral, since it implies that we can sometimes agree to do evil if it becomes necessary for our personal gain.

These two speeches show that Macbeth believes in keeping up appearances by behaving morally, but that, when such behavior conflicts with his purpose, he is prepared to sacrifice morality.

ACT I • SCENE 5

Question 1.

How does Shakespeare make Lady Macbeth's first entrance dramatic?

Answer

The physical energy of this woman is evident as she comes

on stage. Her first words after reading the letter suggest that a new source of power and determination has appeared in the drama. Her soliloquy reveals a knowledge of her husband and a determination to drive him to remove all obstacles to the kingship. The calm reading aloud of the letter is contrasted with the energy with which she proclaims:

> Glamis thou art, and Cawdor, and shalt be
> What thou art promised.

She doubts her husband's firmness and makes us feel that she will ensure that he does what she requires of him. This forceful behavior makes her first entrance dramatic.

Question 2.
How does Lady Macbeth differ in disposition from her husband?

Answer
Lady Macbeth is direct in her approach to problems. She is practical and more "realistic" than her husband. She lacks Macbeth's imagination and his habit of debating a proposition before committing himself to it. To his wife, Macbeth seems indecisive because of weakness or cowardice. She does not sympathize with him or his fears and principles. She has the stronger character, and this causes the undoing of both of them.

She speaks in bold, absolute terms:

> Come, you spirits
> That tend on mortal thoughts, unsex me here,
> And fill me, from the crown to the toe, top-full
> Of direst cruelty! make thick my blood,
> Stop up the access and passage to remorse,
> That no compunctious visitings of nature
> Shake my fell purpose, . . .

It is not surprising, then, that Lady Macbeth previously declared:

> yet do I fear thy [Macbeth's] nature;
> It is too full o' the milk of human kindness.

36

Both Macbeth and his wife are ambitious and superstitious, yet she seems to be naturally more ruthless and less sensitive to guilt than he is. He becomes ruthless and indulges in unnecessary killing later on, but she leads him in this direction.

Question 3.

What purposes are served by (a) the letter with which Scene 5 opens; (b) the first soliloquy of this scene; (c) the soliloquy beginning at line 35?

Answer

(a) The letter presents Lady Macbeth and informs us that Macbeth has told her of the prospect of his becoming king. The letter also reveals the close relationship between these two characters.

(b) The first soliloquy reveals Lady Macbeth's nature, indicates that direct action will probably be taken to make Macbeth king and reveals that she knows her husband's weaknesses and is prepared to strengthen his courage when it fails.

(c) We learn that, while she is ruthless and direct, Lady Macbeth is not quite lacking in human feeling. She has, however, inner resources that enable her to overcome her pangs of conscience. The end of this speech indicates that she will be the leader in this venture. At this point, she even considers "doing the deed" herself.

Question 4.

Comment on the expression, "too full o' the milk of human kindness," as applied to Macbeth.

Answer

It has been pointed out that the sense of this passage would be more obvious if the phrase, "human kindness," were printed as one word, "humankind-ness." We are not to presume that Macbeth was remarkable for kindness to others, but rather that, in the opinion of his wife, he was of too ordinary a nature to perform any uncommon or unnatural deed.

Question 5.

How do you reconcile Lady Macbeth's speech, ("He that's coming . . .) in lines 66-70 with the eventual murder of Duncan by Macbeth?

Answer

Lady Macbeth sounds as though she means to kill Duncan herself. However, it would be dramatically inappropriate for anyone but Macbeth to perform the actual murder. Lady Macbeth's statement reveals her strength and determination and indicates that she knows how to lead Macbeth on. In this speech, some of her resolution is being transmitted to him.

ACT I • SCENE 6

Question 1.

How do you account for Macbeth's not being present to greet the king on his arrival at the castle?

Answer

Macbeth may lack the courage to face his intended victim, King Duncan. He is, perhaps, off by himself, considering whether to murder Duncan.

Question 2.

In Scene 5, Lady Macbeth advised her husband to "look like the innocent flower, but be the serpent under it." What speeches in Scene 6 indicate that she is skilful at putting into practice her own advice?

Answer

Lady Macbeth is an accomplished actress. With perfect hypocrisy, she disguises her true feelings when she welcomes King Duncan with the speech beginning, "All our service. . . ." She continues in the same manner with the speech, "Your servants ever. . . ." No one would be able to detect in her words, so full of humble courtesy and respect, her evil intent.

Question 3.

Point out at least three instances of dramatic irony in Scene 6.

Answer

In his first speech, Duncan reveals that he is perfectly unaware of the treachery awaiting him in the castle. Duncan innocently comments on the "pleasant seat" of Inverness, not realizing the doom that awaits him there.

In line 10, the audience knows that Lady Macbeth is not, as

the king describes her, an "honour'd hostess," but Duncan does not suspect her.

In line 23, Duncan sincerely believes in Macbeth's "great love" for him, but, again, the audience is aware of his error.

The element of double meaning runs through all three examples of dramatic irony cited above.

Question 4.
Why does Shakespeare devote such a large part of Scene 6 to portraying Duncan's appreciation of beauty, his innocence, graciousness and generosity?

Answer
Shakespeare makes Duncan appear so civilized and human in order to make the murder of this gentle king even more horrible. Had he been less admirable, the deed would have seemed less shocking. If Duncan had been an evil king, his death would have come as the logical consequence of his own actions. One villain would have overthrown another. Considering Duncan's kind nature, it is understandable why Macbeth hesitates to murder him. Duncan's appreciation of beauty, his innocence, graciousness and generosity are displayed to plant doubts in the mind of even such a determined military man as Macbeth.

ACT I • SCENE 7
Question 1.
Examine the soliloquy with which Scene 7 opens in order to find out why Macbeth hesitates to murder Duncan.

Answer
This soliloquy stresses Macbeth's fear of punishment in this world. He is prepared to suffer for eternity, if only his ambition may go unpunished in this life. The latter part of the speech recognizes certain moral obstacles on Macbeth's part to killing his relative, his king and his guest. Also, Duncan's innocence is a factor that protects him. While Macbeth may be just rationalizing, he recognizes danger in committing a crime that will turn the nation against the man responsible.

Question 2.
How does Lady Macbeth drive Macbeth to the point where

he will consent to murder Duncan? How is her final argument consistent with Macbeth's reflection at the beginning of his long soliloquy in this scene?

Answer
First, she accuses him of cowardice, an excellent approach when speaking to the greatest soldier in Scotland. Then, she assures him that the crime will go undetected by outlining the details for him. This persuades him, since it seems that, for Macbeth, the consequences of "judgment here" are the main considerations holding him back.

Question 3.
How does the last scene of Act I end the conflict that has been going on in Macbeth's mind since his first appearance in Scene 3?

Answer
One can trace Macbeth's indecision and hesitation from Scene 3. He longs to hear more predictions from those "imperfect speakers," the witches, and says that he "would they had stayed." When informed that he is thane of Cawdor, he mentions "the greatest" prediction that is "behind" and the possibility of murder to come. His hope that "chance" will make him king is destroyed when he hears Malcolm proclaimed prince. Then, he contemplates murder again. Undecided, he returns to his castle and promises to "speak further" with Lady Macbeth. In Scene 7, his wife finally convinces him to make up his mind. On this note of resolution, the scene ends.

Question 4.
How does the dramatist give the last speech of Scene 7 a note of finality that also rounds out the whole of Act I?

Answer
All Macbeth's indecision ends with this last speech of the act. The statement, "I am settled," and the decision to play the required role of deception achieve a rounding out of the whole of Act I, a definiteness that sends us into Act II knowing that if Act I was concerned with Macbeth's temptation and his giving in to it, Act II will be concerned with the crime itself.

ACT II • SCENE 1

Question 1.
Describe the setting for Scene 1.

Answer

This is an interesting setting for the scene preceding the murder and for the murder scene itself, for the murder does not take place on stage. We see the courtyard of Macbeth's castle at Inverness. It is night, and torchlight creates light and shadow. The darkness, the cold, the gray walls and the flickering torchlight combine to produce an atmosphere of fearfulness and evil as Macbeth utters his dagger soliloquy.

Question 2.
What dramatic purposes are served by: (a) Banquo's speech, lines 4-8 (b) the conversation between Banquo and Macbeth (c) the dagger soliloquy?

Answer

(a) This speech suggests that Banquo has a sense of approaching disaster and that, even in his dreams, he cannot resist worrying about evil. Unlike Macbeth in his waking hours, Banquo cannot dismiss such thoughts.

(b) There is a contrast between the forced remarks of Macbeth and the more natural speech of Banquo. In lines 26-29, Banquo is guarded in his words, evidently recognizing that Macbeth is possibly not to be trusted.

(c) The dagger speech is an appropriate introduction to Macbeth's climbing the stairs to murder Duncan, as it achieves the proper emotional tension for both Macbeth and the audience. Of course, a man who is seeing daggers in the air is not the ideal type to carry out a murder, for he is too imaginative and emotional to remain undetected in his crime. We wonder how such a man will conduct himself during and after the crime.

Question 3.
Why is Banquo reluctant to go to bed?

Answer

He is fighting against the temptations of the witches. In his sleep, he is powerless to resist their horrible suggestions. Last night, he dreamed of them. Only by painful and continued wakefulness can he avoid a recurrence of his awful dreams.

Question 4.

Should the dagger seen by Macbeth be visible to the audience?

Answer

The point may be argued either way. Some favor seeing it, since most audiences need the visual aid, not being able to imagine it. Most are opposed to seeing it, since there is no dagger in the air, except in Macbeth's imagination.

Question 5.

Scene 1 of Act II advances the action of the plot little, if at all. What loss, however, would result if this scene were omitted when the play is performed?

Answer

If it is to be a powerful emotional experience for the audience, a murder must be prepared for. Raised to the proper tension as Macbeth fearfully creeps across the stone courtyard to the horrifying sound of the bell, the audience is in the proper mental state for the events of Scene 2.

Question 6.

Comment on the effectiveness of the ending of this scene.

Answer

This is a powerful ending. Macbeth's unsuccessful effort to act naturally with Banquo is followed by a speech that shows him to be highly disturbed. He sees the dagger, yet cannot grasp it. He imagines that he sees blood on it and begins to express a highly imaginative concept of murder (personified) at work. The bell sounded by Lady Macbeth forces him to move toward Duncan's room. In that setting and atmosphere, the slow, fearful exit of Macbeth is most effective.

ACT II • SCENE 2
Question 1.
Describe Macbeth's mental state after the murder.

Answer

Macbeth is horrified by what he has just done. His speech is incoherent and full of distress. He seems to have undergone some sort of mental collapse. He is haunted by visions of guilt and punishment. We see him now as a man who deserves some pity. His earlier strength becomes weakness under his present burden of guilt. This instability contrasts with the firmness and stability of Lady Macbeth.

Question 2.

How is Scene 2 the climax of events so far in the play?

Answer

From Macbeth's meeting with the witches in Act I, Scene 3, events have pointed toward this scene, in which Duncan is killed. The witches' prophecy encouraged Macbeth to consider the kingship; Lady Macbeth supported him further in pursuing this ambition; and, finally, Macbeth decides for himself to murder to gain his ends. In the sense that this scene sums up an event that has been prepared for, it is the climax of the tragedy so far.

Question 3.

Why does Duncan's murder not take place on-stage?

Answer

There are various dramatic advantages to having this murder performed off-stage: some of Lady Macbeth's nervous tension is transmitted to the audience, and suspense is created as we wait to see if the murder is committed and, if so, how Macbeth will act afterward. Extra touches, such as Macbeth's involuntary cry in line 8 and his vivid description of his experience, are only possible when the murder is committed off-stage. Killing off-stage conforms to the ancient Greek tragic tradition requiring a report and, therefore, a reporter of the terrible deed. In this scene, Macbeth reports his own deed. It has additional authority coming from him, and this adds to the dramatic effectiveness.

Question 4.

How do Macbeth and Lady Macbeth react to the murder?

Answer

Lady Macbeth, nervous during the minutes of waiting, has

control of herself after Macbeth reappears. Macbeth lacks this self-control. His behavior is in line with his mental state immediately before the murder. Seeing his condition, she summons all her strength to help him regain control over himself: he must not face his servants and friends in an unusual emotional state. She is able to return the daggers to the death-chamber, an act that turns out to have been beyond his power.

Question 5.
Show that Macbeth is more imaginative than his wife.

Answer
In their conversation after the murder, Macbeth "wastes himself in vague imaginative remorse," while his wife keeps her thoughts strictly to the matter in hand. She is practical and wastes no words. Her powerful will keeps her from thinking the thoughts that she feels would make her mad. Macbeth appears to have no will and no control over his imagination.

Question 6.
What is the effect of the increasingly loud knocking heard toward the end of this scene?

Answer
The knocking, growing louder with each repetition, sounds so demanding and frightening when heard against that setting and in that situation that the audience is keyed up again for what is to follow. The Macbeths have to act quickly because of this sudden interference with their deed. We wonder if Macbeth will have time to react properly to the discovery of Duncan's corpse.

Question 7.
On what note does Scene 2 end?

Answer
Scene 2 ends on a note of regret on Macbeth's part for having "done the deed." He had not anticipated this reaction. In the light of his remorse, his previous words "If it were done . . . then it were well it were done quickly" become ironic.

44

ACT II • SCENE 3

Question 1.

(a) Discuss the humor of the porter's speech. (b) Why is this speech in prose rather than verse? (c) What dramatic purposes are served by this speech?

Answer

(a) The humor lies partly in his drunken actions and speech and partly in the fiction of the interesting people that he might meet if he were in the position of being porter at the gate of hell.

(b) The porter, being a humble workingman, normally would talk in prose in a play by Shakespeare. His drunken condition would make poetry seem further out of place in this context.

(c) This speech enables the Macbeths to prepare for the waking of the castle. Lady Macbeth had directed Macbeth to put on his dressing gown, and this scene gives him time to do that. Also, the speech, because of its humor, relieves tension, which has been high for two scenes and is to rise again almost immediately.

Question 2.

In Act I, Scene 3, 137-8, Macbeth said:

Present fears
Are less than horrible imaginings.

Present evidence from this scene and from earlier parts of the play to show that the statement holds true in his case.

Answer

The most obvious example of "horrible imaginings" occurs in the dagger speech. But in the discovery of the murder scene, where we find Macbeth faced with a concrete situation, he acts out his deception quite well. We find no evidence of the terror that gripped him in the murder scene. The actual situation finds the great soldier conducting himself well, in contrast to the time when his imagination ran wild.

Question 3.

How is Macbeth's speech (lines 92-102) in keeping with his character and customary behavior?

Answer

A highly imaginative man, Macbeth is carried away as he begins what he probably intended to be a factual answer. The speech develops into a vivid and poetic account of the murdered king. We have previously heard such poetic passages in his "farewell" to sleep and in the dagger speech.

Question 4.

Comment on the behavior of Macbeth and his wife after the discovery.

Answer

Notice that Macbeth plays his part better than Lady Macbeth does. Macbeth shows all the signs of sorrow for Duncan's death; his wife almost betrays herself by showing too much concern that the murder was committed under her roof. Had she been innocent, nothing but the murder would have affected her. However, Macbeth's expressions of grief are extravagant and unnatural and they contrast with the spontaneous cries of passion of the other characters.

Question 5.

What do Banquo, Lennox, Macduff, Malcolm and Donalbain do or say in this scene that is a bad sign for the future of Macbeth?

Answer

Banquo's "Too cruel anywhere" speech reveals his suspicion of Lady Macbeth's "What, in our house" remark. More important, in lines 112-118, he takes a definite stand against treason. Lennox's "as it seemed" (line 86) indicates that he doubts the servants' guilt. Macduff, who wants to know why Macbeth killed the grooms, takes his stand with Banquo against "treasonous malice." Malcolm and Donalbain, suspecting treason in the least likely places, decide to save themselves by leaving Scotland. To them; "the near in blood, the nearer bloody," such as Macbeth, are dangerous.

Question 6.

Show how Malcolm and Donalbain play into Macbeth's hands.

Answer

Their flight, as we see in the next scene, "puts upon them suspicion of the deed." Had they stood their ground, they might have found supporters, and the truth might have come out.

ACT II • SCENE 4

Question 1.

In Scene 4, what strange omens are said to have accompanied the murder of Duncan? In what other play by Shakespeare have you found nature portrayed as being disturbed over human behavior?

Answer

Darkness blots out the sun; a falcon is killed by an owl; and Duncan's horses turn wild and are reported to have bitten or eaten one another. Nature is disturbed over human behavior in the storm scene in *Julius Caesar,* before the Battle of Shrewsbury in *Henry IV,* Part I and in the storm scenes in *King Lear,* although, in this last case, the storm seems to be paralleling and emphasizing the events of the play. In *Macbeth,* the falcon might represent Duncan, the owl Macbeth. The sun would represent fair government and civic harmony, which are destroyed (blotted out) by evil (darkness), or, again, Duncan (the sun) and Macbeth.

Question 2.

Why is Macduff's decision to go to Fife rather than Scone of dramatic importance?

Answer

Macduff's decision to ride to Fife is his first act of defiance against Macbeth. Macbeth has gone to Scone to be crowned. Macduff's decision not to be present at the coronation represents the beginning of opposition to Macbeth and what he has come to stand for.

Question 3.

Discuss Macbeth's claim to the throne of Scotland.

Answer

After the death of Duncan, Malcolm would, in the ordinary course of events, ascend to the throne. By fleeing, he and Donalbain practically abandon their claim. Macbeth, being next in relationship to Duncan, for they were cousins (Act I, Scene 4), is naturally selected to fill the vacant throne.

ACT III • SCENE 1

Question 1.
What is the purpose of soliloquies in Shakespeare's plays? Briefly state the general tone of Macbeth's soliloquy in this scene.

Answer
Shakespeare's soliloquies enable the reader to gain insight into the character and private thoughts of the important characters of the drama.

The predominant note of this soliloquy is Macbeth's fear of Banquo — a fear that stems from a sense of moral inferiority. Macbeth's deterioration is made clear. He acknowledges to himself that he has sold himself to the powers of evil, and he resolves to allow no obstacle to stand in the way of his ambition.

Question 2.
What dramatic purposes did Shakespeare achieve by having Macbeth hire murderers for his second major crime, rather than carry it through himself?

Answer
The hiring of murderers indicates a "loosening" in Macbeth's attitude toward crime. Also, he plots this crime without Lady Macbeth's knowledge and approval. She might have advised a different course.

Question 3.
How does Macbeth convince the murderers to murder Banquo?

Answer
He arouses their anger by telling them that it was Banquo who had prevented them from rising in the world. Then, Macbeth scorns their lack of courage. He assures them, finally that he will plan the details of the murder. Therefore, Macbeth is clever enough to get them emotionally involved in the task that he wants them to perform. He then succeeds in giving them a motive for performing it.

Question 4.
How is Macbeth's decision to murder Fleance of special dramatic significance?

Answer
This decision is related to the fact that Macbeth detests the prospect of having Banquo's heirs benefit from what he has done. Macbeth's decision goes back to the prediction of the witches about Banquo. It may also be related to the fact that Fleance would be obligated to avenge his father's death. By having father and son killed, Macbeth hopes to make his future more secure.

ACT III • SCENE 2
Question 1.
What change has come over Lady Macbeth since Act I in her attitude toward wrongdoing and in her treatment of Macbeth?

Answer
Lines 4-7 reveal her sorrow for wrongdoing and a realization that she and Macbeth have not attained happiness with power and position. This is a line of thought that she had not considered before urging Macbeth to kill Duncan.

Now she reasons with Macbeth, but without the force exhibited in Act I and in Act II, Scene 2. She realizes Macbeth is getting beyond her control when she exclaims, "You must leave this." Whereas Lady Macbeth had been the leader earlier, Macbeth is the leader now.

Question 2.
What is the significance of the fact that Macbeth does not tell his wife of his intention to murder Banquo?

Answer
Having begun a career of evil, Macbeth must now go on to commit further crimes. He has discovered that the murder of Duncan is not enough, and he plans to go further so that he may live in peace. Now he plots his own course. It is dramatically and psychologically necessary that he do this on his own. He no longer needs his wife's advice or support. It is not possible for him to turn back, or even to stand still now. He has reached the point of no return.

Question 3.

Is Macbeth's behavior based on conscience or fear?

Answer

Fear is the basis of Macbeth's behavior — fear arising from insecurity. He cannot be content until he is certain that his claim to the throne will remain undisputed, during his lifetime and afterward. However, although Lady Macbeth says she has "given suck," there is no sign elsewhere in the play that she and Macbeth have any children who might be heirs to the throne.

ACT III • SCENE 3

Question 1.

Where in Scene 3 would you place the crisis, or turning point, of the plot? What problem faced Shakespeare in this play, in which the crisis falls as early as the mechanical middle of the play?

Answer

The crisis, or turning point, is usually placed at the point at which Banquo is killed, but Fleance escapes. The death of Banquo marks the end of Macbeth's successes, the peak of the rising action. Fleance's escape represents the first major setback that Macbeth encounters.

Shakespeare's problem in having the dramatic crisis occur near the mechanical middle of the play was that he had a long falling action, almost half the play, in which he had to sustain the audience's interest.

Question 2.

Is there any reason for supposing that the third murderer introduced in this scene is Macbeth in disguise?

Answer

Macbeth would naturally wish to spy upon the actions of the murderers, and he would be unable to trust anyone but himself. The third murderer is better acquainted than the others with the customs of the court (lines 12-14) and he is the first to recognize Banquo. He assumes the leadership of the band and is the first to notice the escape of Fleance.

ACT III • SCENE 4

Question 1.

Show that Shakespeare represented the ghost of Banquo as being visible only to Macbeth.

Answer

Macbeth sees that all chairs are occupied when Lennox says "Here is a place reserved, sir." The lords exclaim, "What, my good lord?" in response to Macbeth's question, "Which of you have done this?" Lady Macbeth says, "You look but on a stool" when Macbeth stares wildly at the ghost.

Question 2.

Should the ghost be visible to the audience? What would be gained or lost by having the ghost on the stage? What staging problems would result if the ghost were visible?

Answer

Usually, the ghost is seen because the visual is always appealing to most members of the audience. However, a director would be perfectly justified in not having a ghost, in which case Banquo's spirit would become simply a figment of Macbeth's imagination. If the ghost does appear in this scene, there are two methods of staging it: The table is placed in such a position that the ghost can come and go behind the guests without their being aware of him; the image of a ghost can be projected on a screen placed on Macbeth's chair by means of a slide projector or even an old-fashioned lantern device. Properly handled, this method can be very effective. This screen ghost can be made to appear and disappear instantaneously.

Question 3.

Is there any reason for supposing that Lady Macbeth is aware of Banquo's murder?

Answer

No. Lady Macbeth has been kept in ignorance of Banquo's murder and she probably thinks that the vision that terrifies Macbeth is the ghost of the murdered Duncan. That Macbeth subsequently informs her of the murder is evident from a later scene (Act V, Scene 1, 62-64).

Question 4.

How have we been prepared earlier in the play for Macbeth's seeing Banquo's ghost and for his complete loss of control over himself?

Answer

The Macbeth who saw the dagger and whose imagination ran away with itself in the murder scene would be likely to lose control of himself in this situation. Such earlier behavior foreshadows his present hallucination.

Question 5.

What differences are observable in the behavior of the ghost and of Macbeth on the two occasions of its appearance?

Answer

On the first occasion, the ghost shakes its head and looks at Macbeth disapprovingly; on the second occasion it glares at Macbeth. After the ghost has vanished for the first time, Macbeth regains his courage and drives the horror from his mind, but on the second occasion, he speaks of it and of his terror to the assembled lords, confirming whatever suspicions they may have already formed.

Question 6.

How does Lady Macbeth attempt to save Macbeth from the desperate situation into which he gets himself in the banquet scene? Why is it dramatically right that she should fail?

Answer

She tries to shame him out of his state, her usual method of dealing with him. It is dramatically right that she should fail on this occasion because her control over him has gone by this time. He must now work out his own destiny alone.

Question 7.

What is the dramatic importance of Macbeth's decision to return to the witches?

Answer

By seeking out the witches, Macbeth gives himself over completely to the forces of evil. Trusting them, he will be led on as they predicted.

Question 8.

How do Macbeth's last two speeches of Act III, Scene 4, reveal the deterioration of his character?

Answer

The two speeches indicate that Macbeth suspects all his noblemen and is probably suspected by them, and that the crimes already committed will seem insignificant compared with those soon to be undertaken. The tragedy of deteriorating character is reflected in these growing suspicions and suggestions of worse crimes to come.

Question 9.

Comment on Lady Macbeth's behavior toward her husband after the guests leave.

Answer

Notice that she is now all tenderness. She does not speak a word of criticism. She knows that Macbeth is doomed by his own weakness. Her only thought is to encourage him to get some sleep, the "balm of hurt minds."

ACT III • SCENE 5

Question 1.

What is the relationship of Hecate to the other three witches?

Answer

Hecate is the queen of the witches and of the underworld. She resents not having been consulted when the other three witches began their interference with Macbeth. Their independent action was a rejection of her authority, and kept her from performing her function — the doing of evil. She is a more potent force than the other witches. Not only can she foresee the future, she can create "magic sleights" to raise spirits that will destroy her victims.

Question 2.

What is the purpose of this scene?

Answer

This scene is further preparation for Macbeth's eventual downfall. That Hecate will now have some influence over Macbeth's fate reinforces the idea that his world will be overturned. She will ensure that he will have a false feeling of security that, in time, will contribute to his tragic ruin.

ACT III • SCENE 6

Question 1.

How is Scene 6 an effective closing scene for Act III?

Answer

As the act closes, forces are gathering against Macbeth. Lennox, probably representative of the thanes, recognizes by his ironic remarks the crimes of Macbeth, and Macduff has defied Macbeth by going to the English court to join forces with Malcolm. Help from England is assured, and hope is strong that Scotland will be relieved of tyranny soon.

ACT IV • SCENE 1

Question 1.

Why is the ritual of the witches in the first scene of this act made even more repulsive than that of Act I, Scene 3?

Answer

Dramatically, it is desirable that the witches should be made more repulsive with each successive appearance. An audience would not stay interested without such an increasing degree of detail and horror. Another reason for this intensification of loathsomeness is the fact that the witches must display more evil power than was necessary at the beginning, as Macbeth's damnation becomes progressively blacker and more involved.

Question 2.

Describe Macbeth's second meeting with the witches.

Answer

He now seeks the witches, who had waited for him before. He has no doubts about their evil nature, being determined "to know, by the worst means, the worst." Any moral hesitation he may once have felt has now entirely left him.

Question 3.
What is signified by each of the three figures that rises from the cauldron to speak to Macbeth?

Answer
The armed head represents Macbeth, whose head is to be cut off by Macduff; the bloody child represents Macduff and foreshadows the statement later of his unnatural birth; the crowned child with the tree in his hand represents Malcolm's order that his soldiers carry branches of Birnam Wood as camouflage for their numbers, and his being crowned king.

Question 4.
How is Macbeth's decision to murder Macduff's family consistent with his developing character?

Answer
Shakespeare wishes to paint a character that exhibits progressive deterioration as the play proceeds. Macbeth had intended to commit one crime and then stop, but he is driven on to commit others. There was some evil logic behind the murder of Banquo; there is no point to the murder of the Macduff family. There is also no attempt at concealment, as there had been earlier. Murder for its own sake has come to dominate the actions of Macbeth, and, obviously, the tragedy of the breakdown of his character is near the end.

ACT IV • SCENE 2
Question 1.
In their judgments of Macduff's flight from Scotland, who is correct, Lady Macduff or Ross?

Answer
One may argue either way. Macduff goes to England with the highest of motives: to obtain help for his country and to associate with Malcolm in an attack against Macbeth. He does not know that Macbeth will murder his family. Lady Macduff, naturally, views her husband's flight as desertion of his family and a mark of cowardice. She is looking at the matter from an emotional, entirely subjective point of view.

Question 2.

What is the purpose of introducing Macduff's son into the play?

Answer

We admire the courage and spirit of the boy, and our confidence is increased in Macduff, the father of so brave a child. The scene presents a visible illustration of the almost inhuman cruelty of Macbeth and consequently destroys any lingering admiration that we may feel for him. Finally, the massacre of Macduff's family angers Macduff and makes him the natural avenger of both his country's wrongs and his private injuries.

Question 3.

What is the dramatic value of the humorous conversation between Lady Macduff and her son?

Answer

On its own merits as humor, this conversation plays well on stage. Dramatically, it relieves the tension between quite tense scenes, and this grim play can stand a little interval of humor.

Question 4.

How does the third major crime of Macbeth differ from the first and second crimes?

Answer

No thought is given to this murder. For the first murder, Macbeth carefully weighed whether he should commit the crime. For the second murder, he spent time in careful planning. But not so in this third murder. Macbeth committed the first murder himself and was closely involved in the second, but, in this case, he simply sent murderers to do the job.

Question 5.

Is there any significance in that fact that Macduff's family is killed in daylight, rather than at night, as Duncan and Banquo were?

Answer

Many of the early scenes are set in gloom or darkness. The

first two murders are carried out at night. Now, Macbeth makes no attempt to conceal his crimes, but boldly has the murders carried out in broad daylight.

ACT IV • SCENE 3

Question 1.
How, and for what purposes, does Malcolm condemn himself in his conversation with Macduff?

Answer
Malcolm is, of course, testing Macduff's loyalty to Scotland and hatred of Macbeth. Also, when he does come out with the truth about himself, he, by contrast, takes on added nobility. We assume that his wisdom and integrity will make him a good king for Scotland.

Question 2.
What dramatic purposes are achieved by this scene?

Answer
Macduff and Malcolm are united against Macbeth. We learn that the English are prepared to help them in an invasion of Scotland. Macduff, on learning of his family's murder, is driven to a decision to avenge that crime and remove the tyrant, Macbeth, from Scotland.

Question 3.
What evidence does this scene offer of Malcolm's fitness to rule?

Answer
Our first impressions of Malcolm undergo a considerable change in the course of the scene. Aside from his own description of his virtues, we observe first that old Siward, a staunch soldier, is ready to serve under him. Then we learn that Malcolm is respected in his own country, where his eye "would create soldiers, make our women fight" (assuming that the lines 179-181 are addressed to Malcolm, who replies to them). Finally, when Malcolm encourages Macduff to seek revenge against Macbeth and speaks in "manly tune," we are ready to accept him as the savior of Scotland.

ACT V • SCENE 1

Question 1.

What association is there between the setting for this scene and the predictions of the apparitions in Act IV, Scene 1?

Answer

The setting of Dunsinane carries us back to the third apparition's promise that Macbeth would not be defeated until Birnam Wood moved to Dunsinane.

Question 2.

To what incidents in her past does Lady Macbeth refer during her sleepwalking?

Answer

The rubbing of the hands is obviously an attempt to remove the blood of Duncan. The "One; two . . . " is a reference to the ringing of the bell. "Fie, my lord, fie, a soldier and afear'd" probably refers to her remarks in the banquet scene, although this statement may go back to Act I, Scene 7. "Put on your nightgown" refers to Act II, Scene 2, 70.

Question 3.

In what scornful way had Lady Macbeth referred to blood in Act II, Scene 2? What is her attitude toward blood now?

Answer

It was she who said, in scorn of Macbeth's fear, "A little water clears us of this deed." Now, of course, the thought of blood terrifies and obsesses her. It brings her mind to the breaking point.

Question 4.

What line in the doctor's final speech of the scene is a preparation for the later news of Lady Macbeth's death "by self and violent hands"?

Answer

"Look after her;/ Remove from her the means of all annoyance," in lines 78-79, foreshadows the eventual suicide.

Question 5.
Define the term, nemesis. What form does nemesis take with Lady Macbeth?

Answer
Nemesis is retributive justice, a fitting punishment for wrongdoing. In Lady Macbeth's case, her punishment is fitting in that her mind, which was so strong when she convinced Macbeth to murder Duncan, has broken down at the end of the tragedy.

ACT V • SCENE 2

Question 1.
How is Siward related to the other characters in the play?

Answer
According to Holinshed, Shakespeare's historical source, "Duncan had two sons by his wife, who was the daughter of Siward, Earl of Northumberland." Act IV, Scene 3, 127-128 and 183-185 describe how Siward is related to Malcolm II.

Question 2.
What is the dramatic function of this scene?

Answer
This brief scene prepares for the coming battle. It is the first of a series of quick, alternating scenes that allow the audience to witness, practically simultaneously, the fortunes of both sides in the battle.

ACT V • SCENE 3

Question 1.
How is this scene a contrast to the preceding scene?

Answer
The hopelessness and despair of Macbeth contrast with the cool determination of his enemies; the hatred of Macbeth's subjects varies with the loyalty of Malcolm's; the rapid changes of mood in Macbeth differ distinctly from the unity and firmness of the Scottish lords.

Question 2.

Compare the Macbeth of Act V, Scene 3 with that of Act I to show the state to which his ambition has brought him.

Answer

The deterioration that has come about in Macbeth's character is evident in Act V. The self-sufficiency and self-control of the man who, in Act I, was Scotland's greatest soldier has been replaced by a man of changing moods, one who boasts one minute and is fearful and downcast the next, one who strikes his servant and shouts at his men, one who hardly knows his own mind, as he has Seyton fasten on his armor and then shouts "Pull't off."

ACT V • SCENE 4

Question 1.

In respect to plot development, which is the most important speech in Scene 4?

Answer

> Let every soldier hew me down a bough
> And bear't before him; thereby shall we shadow
> The numbers of our host

This is the key speech, since Birnam Wood is, in a sense, about to move to Dunsinane, as predicted.

Question 2.

How does this scene begin to renew our sympathy for Macbeth?

Answer

We see the sad trick that the weird sisters have played on Macbeth and we begin to feel that, despite his villainy, Macbeth is also a victim of the supernatural forces of evil, which have been using him for their own ends.

ACT V • SCENE 5

Question 1.

In this scene, what further disastrous news for Macbeth follows that of the queen's death?

Answer

Macbeth learns that Birnam Wood has been seen moving, and he realizes that the third apparition had deceived him when it promised him safety until Birnam Wood moved to Dunsinane.

Question 2.

How are we made to feel pity and admiration for Macbeth in this scene?

Answer

We pity this man for the situation he has brought on himself. It is always pathetic to see a great man turn from good to evil. We admire him for his courage as he, with his wife dead and his world collapsing around him, resolves to fight to the end and die "with harness on his back."

ACT V • SCENE 6

Question 1.

What appears to be the purpose of this short scene?

Answer

During the first half of the play, we may have formed the impression that Malcolm was inefficient and powerless to cope with such a general as Macbeth. In Act I, Scene 2, we learned that he narrowly escaped capture, from which he was saved by the sergeant. Later, we saw him "shifting away" (Act II, Scene 3). Later still, we saw him, with almost excessive caution, test the loyalty of Macduff. But Shakespeare would not raise a character to the throne of Scotland without showing that character to be worthy of the noble and difficult position that he is called to occupy. Consequently, Shakespeare has taken care to raise Malcolm in the estimation of the audience, and we now see him using the imperial "we" and confidently issuing instructions to such men as Siward, Siward's son and "worthy Macduff."

ACT V • SCENE 7

Question 1.

What is the dramatic importance of the fight between Macbeth and young Siward?

Answer

This is the last touch of rising action in the midst of a

generally falling action. As Macbeth kills young Siward, his faith in the second apparition's statement that no man born of woman would harm him is revived. Thus, the fight with Macduff will take on increased interest.

Question 2.
Why is it desirable to have Macduff appear toward the end of this scene?

Answer
His appearance and expressed determination to seek out only Macbeth in the battle foreshadows their climactic fight in the closing scene.

Question 3.
Old Siward says, "the castle's gently render'd." If the battle is over, why will Scene 8 not be an anti-climax?

Answer
We are not especially interested in the battle, except for its relation to Macbeth. We are interested in Macbeth and in seeing what form the tragedy concerning him will take. Everything pointed to the invaders' victory in the battle; therefore, we are not surprised when they actually win. Now we are looking ahead to the meeting of Macbeth and Macduff and wondering about the prediction of the second apparition.

ACT V • SCENE 8
Question 1.
Why does Macbeth try to avoid Macduff in the battle?

Answer
Macbeth is not afraid of death at the hands of Macduff. He is, rather, afraid of killing Macduff. This sentiment is the last spark of nobility in the once great, now hated, warrior, who is genuinely anxious to spare the life of one whom he has already wounded.

Question 2.
Why is the death of Macbeth not presented on the stage?

Answer

Dramatic effect is seldom increased by butchery on-stage. Macbeth's being driven off-stage suggests his certain defeat, and the audience can imagine the death blows and cutting off of the tyrant's head. Since Macduff must show Macbeth's head to the other thanes and to Malcolm, it could not be cut off on the stage.

Question 3.

How does Malcolm's closing speech provide an effective closing for the play?

Answer

With Malcolm hailed as king to replace the tyrant who had brought such bloodshed to Scotland, we feel that a better order is to be introduced. From Act IV, Scene 3, on, we knew that Malcolm would be a good king when placed in that position. He fittingly elevates the thanes to earls, promises that the exiles shall be brought home and the guilty associates of Macbeth punished, informs us of Lady Macbeth's suicide and indicates that he will soon be crowned at Scone.

Part C: General Review Questions and Answers

Question 1.
From what sources did Shakespeare derive this play? Where does he depart from his historical authority?

Answer
Shakespeare derived his material for this play from Ralph Holinshed's *Chronicle of Englande, Irelande, and Scotlande,* published in 1577. Holinshed's narrative is taken from the 12th book of the *Scotorum Historia* of Hector Boece, which was printed in 1526 and translated into the Scottish dialect in 1541. The details concerning the witches, their powers and their practices seem to have been taken from Scot's *Discovery of Witchcraft,* 1584.

The following dramatic episodes in the play are the poet's own creation: (1) The actual murder of the king by Macbeth, together with the incident of the imaginary dagger preceding it. In Holinshed, King Duff is murdered by servants. (2) The appearance of Banquo's ghost at the feast. In Holinshed, Banquo was not murdered until after the banquet. (3) The sleepwalking scene of Lady Macbeth. (4) The slaying of Macbeth by Macduff. (5) The apparitions shown by the witches to Macbeth. (6) The suicide of Lady Macbeth.

Shakespeare departs from the *Chronicle* in several ways:

(1) Duncan speaks in Act I, Scene 1, as though he were not present at the battle with the Norwegian king. Holinshed says, "The king himself governed in the main battle." Shakespeare no doubt wished to emphasize the contrast between the mildness of Duncan's disposition and the energetic nature of Macbeth.

(2) Several historical incidents — the invasion of Sweyn, the rebellion of Macdonwald and a subsequent rebellion — are telescoped into one battle, which we hear of in the second scene. The purpose of this is to concentrate our attention on one point of time and also to add to the picture of Macbeth's great power. For the latter reason, Shakespeare makes Macbeth kill Macdonwald in personal combat, whereas, according to Holinshed, Macdonwald returned to his castle and committed suicide.

(3) According to Holinshed, Macbeth revealed his "purposed intent" (to murder the king) to his "trusty friends,

amongst whom Banquo was the chiefest," and "upon confidence of their promised aid he slew the king at Inverness." In the play, Macbeth's attempt to have Banquo join in his treason utterly fails. The character of Banquo, as Shakespeare portrays it, makes any other result impossible.

Question 2.

Show that, in his scenes of enchantment, Shakespeare has conformed to common superstitions and traditions of his times.

Answer

(1) "There's luck in odd numbers" is still a popular saying, and we constantly observe in the play the use of the magical three and its multiples:

> Act I, Scene 1, 1: "When shall we *three* meet again?"
> Act I, Scene 3, 22: "Weary sen'nights *nine* times nine."
> Act IV, Scene 1, 1: "*Thrice* the brinded cat hath mew'd,
> *Thrice* and once the hedge-pig whined."

(2) Witches were supposed to possess almost unlimited power in producing evil and in drawing people on to destruction, although, according to the popular notion, they could only harm those whose own evil instincts caused them to believe in the wicked suggestions of the evil one. Shakespeare seems to have been showing this by contrasting Macbeth's behavior with that of Banquo under the witches' influence.

(3) According to Scot, witches were supposed to have familiar spirits, who possessed a certain amount of power over them and took the visible forms of animals, such as cats (usually lacking the tail) or toads. So in Act I, Scene 1, the first witch answers the summons of Graymalkin (a cat), and the second of Paddock (a toad).

(4) They supposedly had the power to "raise haile, tempests, and hurtful weather." Therefore, in the play, they always appear in a thunderstorm.

(5) They also could "passe from place to place in the air invisible." This is how they vanish in Act IV, Scene 1, 133. They

are invisible to Lennox, who enters the cave immediately after, and who, Macbeth thinks, must have met them.

(6) They were supposed to foretell future events. Shakespeare's witches foretell the fates of Macbeth and promise Banquo that his heirs shall be kings.

(7) According to popular belief, witches rode the sea in a "riddle or cive." In *Macbeth,* the first witch declares her intention of sailing "in a sieve" to Aleppo (Act I, Scene 3, 8).

(8) In the threat that the sailor shall "dwindle, peak and pine," there is a clear reference to the superstitious use of wax figures of those whom they were intended to injure. These figures were melted by fire in order that those whom they represented might "dwindle, peak and pine" as the wax disappeared.

(9) A lunar eclipse was commonly believed to be a sign of disaster. Thus, we find among the horrible ingredients of the cauldron "slips of yew sliver'd in the moon's eclipse." (Act IV, Scene 1, 27)

(10) The physical appearance of the witches, as described by Banquo, with their skinny lips, choppy fingers and beards, conforms to the popular notions of the age.

(11) Witches were supposed to travel on broomsticks and to hold meetings at which strange ceremonies were performed. Their meetings were accompanied by foul and criminal performances. The witches in *Macbeth* meet in a cavern, or on a "blasted heath," carry on their work with all kinds of terrible instruments, and mix their "hell-broth" with repulsive ingredients.

(12) Finally, witches were dreaded by all. Even Macbeth despises the three, calling them "secret, black, and midnight hags." (Act IV, Scene 1, 48)

Question 3.

Define the term, local color. Is there any evidence in the play that Shakespeare ever visited Scotland?

Answer

Local color refers to details of speech, dress, mannerisms and setting that a writer uses to capture the atmosphere of a particular place. Thus, the wild, barren heath, where the witches meet Macbeth, and the accompanying thunder and lightning, create a sense of weird horror that is appropriate to the treatment of the supernatural and unnatural crime in this play. This atmosphere of weirdness and gloom is maintained throughout the play. The frequent references to night and the creatures of night, the darkness illuminated by the glare of torches in the courtyard of Macbeth's castle, the cavern in which Macbeth seeks the weird sisters, and the dimly burning candle of the sleepwalking scene are details that contribute to the creation of the grim atmosphere.

Shakespeare's portrayal of Scottish manners and superstitions, the Scottish character and the Scottish scenery might lead one to suppose that he had visited Scotland. However, no definite conclusion can be drawn from the local coloring or the knowledge of the land displayed by Shakespeare in the play. The poet's imagination may have supplied the local color, or it may have been derived from various secondary sources.

Question 4.

What are some actual events that occurred in Scotland during the period to which *Macbeth* relates?

Answer

In 1031, Malcolm II of Scotland came to England to pay his respects to Canute. Malcolm was accompanied by two chieftains, one of whom was Macbeode, maormor (underchieftain) of Moray. This is the first recorded mention of Macbeth. He married Gruoch, daughter of Boete and granddaughter of Kenneth IV, who had been killed in battle in 1003 by Malcolm II. He thus strengthened his claim to the throne, being the grandson of Malcolm II by his daughter, Doada. In 1032, Malcolm II murdered the head of Gruoch's house. In 1034, he died and was succeeded by Duncan MacCrinan, his grandson and Macbeth's cousin. At his succession, Duncan chose his son, Malcolm Canmore, to be his heir. Macbeth, seeing all possibility of his succeeding naturally to the crown thus removed, was upset. Duncan's reign was not very successful. He invaded England without gaining anything and, afterwards, started a war with Thorfinn, the Norwegian earl of Orkney. Macbeth was, at that time, a commander in Duncan's army, but his joining with Thorfinn caused Duncan to be murdered at Bothgowan in 1039. Then, through his own claim and through that of his wife, Macbeth took over the Scottish throne.

Macbeth had a properous reign of 17 years. He was a moderate, just, firm and energetic ruler. He encountered a strong enemy in Siward, earl of Northumberland, who invaded Scotland by land and sea in 1054, with the support of Edward the Confessor. On July 27 of the same year, Macbeth was defeated by Siward at the head of an English army. Siward's son, Osborn, and his nephew, Siward, were killed in the battle. Though Malcolm Canmore was proclaimed king, Macbeth retained the crown for some time, probably until 1057, when he was defeated and killed by Macduff in Aberdeenshire. Macbeth's son (or stepson) was raised to the throne, but his reign was short. He was defeated and killed the following year, and Malcolm succeeded to the throne.

Question 5.

"Macbeth is endowed with an imagination of unusual intensity." Illustrate this statement briefly by describing three occasions on which his imagination is particularly active.

Answer

Macbeth's unusually intense imagination is revealed, first, when he sees a dagger (a hallucination) in front of him, the handle toward his hand, in Act II, Scene 1, shortly before he receives the death signal from Lady Macbeth. He admits that he has a powerful imagination when he asks:

or art thou but
A dagger of the mind, a false creation,
Proceeding from the heat-oppressed brain?

Macbeth's imagination is also unusually active in Act III, Scene 4, when he enters the banquet hall and complains that "the table's full." Macbeth thinks he sees the ghost of Banquo (recently murdered at Macbeth's orders) and shouts, "never shake/Thy gory locks at me." This vision is another hallucination.

A third occasion on which Macbeth displays an overactive imagination is when, after hearing from Lennox that Macduff has fled to join Malcolm in England, he decides to "crown" his "thoughts with acts" and murder the Macduff family:

His wife, his babes, and all unfortunate souls
That trace him in his line.

There would have been a logic to killing Macduff, but there is no sense in Macbeth's killing Lady Macduff and her children. This deed does not stem from Macbeth's reason, but rather from his imagination.

Question 6.

Referring to three different scenes in *Macbeth,* discuss the bleeding sergeant's statement about the central character:

For brave Macbeth — well he deserves that name

Answer

Bravery is shown by Macbeth during the battle against the Norwegian invaders (reported by the sergeant in Act I, Scene 2) when, "with his brandish'd steel," he "carved out his passage / Till he faced the slave; And fix'd his head upon our battlements." This deed illustrates military heroism.

In Act I, Scene 7, Macbeth swears to Lady Macbeth that he "dare do all that may become a man; / Who dares do more, is none." Shortly before this, Macbeth had spoken to his wife about "proceeding no further in this business." His defiance of his wife is courageous in the highest sense of that term, for he follows his conscience. For a moment, he displays moral bravery, but it is short-lived.

In Act V, Scene 7, Macbeth, now alone, dismisses the notion of ending his own life with his sword:

Why should I play the Roman fool, and die
On mine own sword? whiles I see lives, the gashes
Do better upon them.

This speech illustrates the desperate courage of the tragic hero, who realizes that he must "try to the last."

Question 7.

Describe the tragic development in the character of Macbeth that leads him to murder King Duncan.

Answer

Macbeth's character undergoes a series of downward steps in the course of his decision to murder Duncan. When we first see

Macbeth, he is a man of honor, respected by his fellow soldiers, especially for his part in the defeat of the rebel forces. However, when he hears the witches' prophecy, he is startled, a reaction showing that he has already considered taking over the throne.

When Macbeth is met by Ross and Angus with the news that he is the new thane of Cawdor, he becomes "rapt" in thought, for one of the witches' prophecies has been fulfilled. He says, in an aside, "Glamis and Thane of Cawdor!/The greatest is behind." At this time, the thought of murder enters his mind. His character has deteriorated to the point where he can visualize himself murdering Duncan, an act:

> Whose horrid image doth unfix my hair,
> And make my seated heart knock at my ribs.

But his deterioration is not yet sufficient to make him decide to commit the murder, for he says:

> If chance will have me king, why, chance may crown
> me
> Without my stir.

The next step in the development of his character is his sudden decision to become king at all costs. When Macbeth hears Duncan's announcement that his son, Malcolm, will be his successor, Macbeth says in a bitter aside:

> that is a step
> On which I must fall down, or else o'erleap,
> For in my way it lies. Stars, hide your fires;
> Let not light see my black and deep desires.

In the soliloquy shortly after Duncan's arrival at Inverness, Macbeth shows that his character has fallen to the point where he is willing to commit the murder, but is afraid of the consequences on earth. He says, "But in these cases/We still have judgment here." If he were assured of safety during his earthly life, he would gladly "jump the life to come."

Finally, when Lady Macbeth has shown Macbeth the way to deal with the practical details of the murder, all his fears vanish and he is no longer troubled by any sense of morality.

This development of character is tragic in that Macbeth, when he first appeared, was a man of noble character, who showed great bravery and physical strength, well illustrated in the sergeant's report to Duncan of Macbeth's conduct in battle. But in Macbeth's character, there is one quality, ambition, that gradually, through a combination of external circumstances (Macbeth's kinship with Duncan and the witches' prophecies), overcomes his good qualities and drives him to destruction.

Question 8.

Define dramatic irony. Describe three examples in *Macbeth* and explain how the dramatic effect is achieved.

Answer

Dramatic irony is a figure of speech or a situation in which a character is made to say or do certain things that are of more significance to other characters or to the audience than they are to him. This device is used in *Macbeth* first, in Act I, Scene 3, when Macbeth enters for the first time with the words:

So foul and fair a day I have not seen.

In his mind, "foul" refers to the weather, "fair" to the battle he has recently won. However, the audience immediately associates these words with the words previously spoken by the witches:

Fair is foul, and foul is fair.

This device, known as echo, is one method of achieving dramatic irony.

A second example of irony occurs when Duncan rides innocently up to Macbeth's castle, commenting that the air:

Nimbly and sweetly recommends itself
Unto our gentle senses.

The audience, knowing what is in Macbeth's mind, knows just what is in store for Duncan later that night. The lack of awareness in Duncan, contrasted with the awareness of Macbeth, Lady Macbeth and the audience, makes this speech dramatically ironic.

71

A third example of dramatic irony occurs in Act II, Scene 3, where the porter innocently imagines himself as the porter at the gates of hell at the very moment when unknown to him, but known to the audience, Duncan's murder is turning the castle of Macbeth into a kind of hell.

Notice that the element of coincidence is common to all three of these examples of dramatic irony.

Question 9.

Discuss the existence of two types of dramatic irony in *Macbeth*: the irony of circumstance or action and the irony of language.

Answer

Irony of circumstance implies a sort of doubledealing in which fate acts in a manner that is the reverse of what we might naturally expect. Such dramatic irony enters largely into the plot of *Macbeth*. The basis of Macbeth's rise to the throne is the witches' promise that he shall be king. The promise is a mocking one; almost immediately, an obstacle arises in Duncan's appointment of Malcolm as prince of Cumberland and his heir. This very obstacle, however, is the means of motivating Macbeth and of leading him to treason. But Macbeth faces still another obstacle. The king is killed, but his sons live, and Macbeth's ambition is still unfulfilled. The flight of Malcolm and Donalbain, however, causes him to be named the successor to the throne. Thus, twice in the action of the play, obstacles have been made to appear, to be used with ironical effect as an unexpected means of fulfilment.

Again, the witches' prophecy with regard to Macduff is an example of ironical action. Macbeth's security has only one obstacle — Macduff. With the view of removing this obstacle, Macbeth decides to destroy Macduff's whole family. His plan succeeds, except for the removal of Macduff himself. The news of the massacre of his family moves Macduff to exclaim:

Front to front
Bring thou this fiend of Scotland and myself;
Within my sword's length set him.

The very means that Macbeth adopts to rid himself of danger become, by the irony of circumstance, the very means by which he falls, since Macduff is determined to have revenge on the murderer of his family.

Irony of language lies in the fact that the audience knows what the actor does not know. The irony consists in ambiguous speech. The actor seems to speak ironically when, in reality, he is only expressing what he thinks to be absolutely true. A few examples will illustrate this form of irony.

In Act I, Scene 4, Duncan remarks:

> There's no art
> To find the mind's construction in the face.
> He was a gentleman on whom I built
> An absolute trust

These words are spoken of the rebellious Cawdor immediately before the entrance of the still more faithless Macbeth. The irony consists in the fact that Duncan is again trusting one who is about to deceive him. Similarly, there is dramatic irony in Duncan's greeting of Macbeth: "O worthiest cousin!" (Act I, Scene 4) Act I contains many more examples of irony. Notice Duncan's remark about the "pleasant seat" of Inverness, the castle in which he will soon be murdered, and his references to Lady Macbeth as his "honour'd hostess" and the "great love, sharp as his spur" Macbeth feels for his king.

Another striking example of the irony of language occurs in Act II, Scene 3. Macduff's concern for Lady Macbeth is, as the audience knows, unnecessary, for she has a hardened, criminal nature:

> O gentle lady,
> 'Tis not for you to hear what I can speak:
> The repetition, in a woman's ear,
> Would murder as it fell.

Also ironic are Macbeth's words in Act III, Scene 4, just before the appearance of Banquo's ghost:

> Here had we now our country's honour roof'd,
> Were the graced person of our Banquo present

Question 10.

Discuss Macbeth's faith in the witches and in their predictions.

Answer

Although Macbeth appears spellbound from the moment of his meeting with the witches, he does not automatically accept their predictions. He is startled by their prophetic greetings because they so exactly express his hopes, but he shows only partial belief in their prophecies.

One part of the prophecy is fulfilled. This strengthens his faith in the second part. Then suspense tempts him to influence the course of events and thus fulfil the predictions. However, overcome by uncertainty, he exclaims:

If chance will have me king, why, chance may crown
me
Without my stir.

Conflicting thoughts run through his mind as he considers the prophecy in favor of Banquo's descendants. In his own case, the sayings of the weird sisters have proved true, and, logically, he should believe that other, undesirable, prediction. He therefore decides to defy fate, and destroy both Banquo and his son.

The escape of Fleance again forces Macbeth to put faith in the witches, though he finds comfort in the thought that "this foe hath no teeth for the present."

After the appearance of Banquo's ghost, Macbeth seeks a second interview with the witches. He decides to join these beings, whom he recognizes to be enemies of God and men. He will believe in them and act as though his faith in them were absolute. In his encounter with Macduff, he discovers the truth of the last prediction of the witches and learns that he has been the blind fool of his own evil desires. Then, for the first time, he realizes that he believed only what he wished to believe about the "juggling fiends":

That keep the word of promise to our ear,
And break it to our hope.

Question 11.

Sketch the characters of Duncan and Malcolm.

Answer

The "meek" and "gracious" Duncan presents a strong con-

74

trast to his vigorous and violent successor to the throne. A man of gentle, trustful and courteous nature, Duncan is too mild and unsuspecting to cope with the restless spirits of his subjects. A successful ruler must at least be able "To find the mind's construction in the face." That Duncan is a good man is evident, but that he is a weak and ineffective ruler is also clear. He chooses the most inappropriate time to make Malcolm prince of Cumberland, and he selects the most dangerous men on whom to build "an absolute trust." But, while we condemn the king, we must also pity the man, whose spotless character Macbeth himself recognizes:

> This Duncan
> Hath borne his faculties so meek, hath been
> So clear in his great office, that his virtues
> Will plead like angels trumpet-tongued, against
> The deep damnation of his taking-off.

The character of Malcolm serves as a foil to that of his trustful father. This contrast is first shown in Malcolm's flight to England after the discovery of Duncan's murder. The same cautious nature, is seen in his interview with Macduff (Act IV, Scene 3). Malcolm's "modest wisdom plucks him from over-credulous haste." However, he has the qualities that make for success. His device of "moving" Birnam Wood ensures success against a difficult enemy. Old Siward is willing to serve under him, and his countrymen will follow him to death. (Act IV, Scene 3, 178-9)

Question 12.
Sketch the character of Banquo, paying particular attention to his connection with the witches.

Answer
The character of Banquo forms a companion picture to that of Macbeth. In courage, energy and service to the people, he resembles Macbeth. Like Macbeth, he possesses a character that appears to be only partially developed. He is honorable, generous, modest, with a preference for what is good over what is not good, yet he never actively exerts himself to set wrong right and, even when his duty is clear, he hesitates so long before tak-

ing action against Macbeth that his former friend has him murdered in the meantime.

He differs from Macbeth in two important respects: in his lack of ambition and in his faith in prayer. Thus, next to Banquo, Macbeth's "Genius is rebuked," for "in his [Banquo's] royalty of nature reigns that which would be fear'd."

Banquo's reaction to the witches is, at first, merely curiosity: "Speak to me who neither beg nor fear your favours nor your hate." He has not had secret ambitions as Macbeth has, and, therefore, the witches' prophecies do not excite him. He is powerfully affected by their words, but he recognizes the witches as "instruments of darkness" that "tell us truths" to "win us to our harms." Consequently, he struggles against the suggestions that they have planted in his mind. That he finds the struggle difficult is evident from his words:

Merciful powers
Restrain in me the cursed thoughts that nature
Gives way to in repose.

He knows that they cannot force him to evil in spite of himself, and he does his utmost to control the ambitious thoughts that they have stirred within him. But he should have done more than this. Knowing that Macbeth was a traitor and a murderer, it was Banquo's duty to his country to act against him, and it was his duty to himself to be on guard against Macbeth. Failing in both these duties, he helped to bring about his country's ruin and his own destruction.

Question 13.
Show the importance of references to night, sleep and dreams in *Macbeth*.

Answer
Night has always been regarded as the time when crimes are committed, when "such bitter business" is done "as the day would quake to look on." At such a time:

Good things of day begin to droop and drowse;
While night's black agents to their preys do rouse.

At night, the powers of evil are supposed to possess the greatest influence, and resistance to temptation to be weakest. Lady Macbeth calls on night to conceal their deeds and prevent heaven from peaking "through the blanket of the dark to cry 'Hold, hold!' " Macbeth plans the murder of Banquo to take place at night, "Ere the bat hath flown/His cloister'd flight." The night of Duncan's murder is "unruly," and is prolonged unnaturally:

> By the clock 'tis day,
> And yet dark night strangles the travelling lamp.

Hecate spends the night before Macbeth's second interview with the witches, preparing to lead him to his ruin: "This night I'll spend unto a dismal and a fatal end."

Sleep is the symbol of peace, peace of body, mind and soul. No wonder, then, that Macbeth feels, in murdering Duncan, that he has murdered his own peace in the form of sleep: "Methought I heard a voice cry 'Sleep no more,' Macbeth doth murder sleep." Even Lady Macbeth is deeply affected by the sight of "innocent sleep." She would, she says, have murdered Duncan with her own hands "Had he not resembled my father as he slept." It is ironic that, while another's sleep prevents her from committing murder, sleep itself is later the means by which she reveals her guilt.

Banquo recognizes the weakness of the will under the influence of sleep (Act II, Scene 1, 7-8), and Lady Macbeth testifies to its value as "tired Nature's sweet restorer" when she says to her husband, "You lack the season of all natures, sleep."

From earliest times, the similarity between sleep and death has been noted by poets. Lady Macbeth says, "the sleeping and the dead are but as pictures." Macduff speaks of sleep as "death's counterfeit," and Macbeth says of Duncan, almost enviously, "After life's fitful fever he sleeps well."

The different references to dreams relate to the theme of the supernatural that runs through the play and determines the course of the action. Banquo's temptation comes to him in dreams: "I dreamt last night of the three weird sisters" he tells Macbeth. "Merciful powers, restrain in me the cursed thoughts that nature gives way to in repose," he also says. These and other allusions indicate that dreams seem to be looked upon as one of the means of transmitting evil. Macbeth speaks of "wicked dreams" that "abuse the curtained sleep." They are sent also as punishments to the guilty. Macbeth sleeps "in the affliction of these terrible dreams that shake us nightly."

Question 14.
Discuss Shakespeare's use of prose and rhymed verse in this play.

Answer
Shakespeare usually uses prose (1) to produce a conversational effect; (2) in light or comic scenes; (3) for letters.

The principal prose passages in *Macbeth* are: (1) Macbeth's letter (Act I, Scene 5); (2) the porter's speech (Act II, Scene 3); (3) Lady Macduff's conversation with her son (Act IV, Scene 2); (4) the sleep-walking scene.

The porter's speech comes closer to comedy than anything else in the play. It serves to give relief to the intensity of the tragedy at this point.

In the conversation between Lady Macduff and her son, a light, natural effect is produced by the use of prose. In the conversation between the doctor and the gentlewoman, in Act V, Scene 1, prose is used because it is in keeping with the domestic surroundings. In this scene, Lady Macbeth also speaks in prose, and the simplicity of style and diction makes the scene impressive.

Except for the witches' parts, which are entirely in verse, Shakespeare uses rhyme in *Macbeth* for the following purposes:
(1) To close a scene, as in Act I, Scene 7:

Away, and mock the time with fairest show,
False face must hide what the false heart doth know.

The rhyming couplet directs attention to the close of a scene. This was important in the days when plays were performed without changes of scenery or dropping of curtains.
(2) To form an effective ending at the end of a speech:

Which shall to all our nights and days to come
Give solely sovereign sway and masterdom.
(Act I, Scene 5)

(3) At the close of a scene or speech that contains a summary

78

of the situation. Rhyme, in this case, ensures that the audience will notice the point. Notice the use of rhyme in the following passage from Act III, Scene 1:

It is concluded: Banquo, thy soul's flight,
If it find heaven, must find it out to-night.

(4) To express a proverbial saying, such as:

Come what may
Time and the hour runs through the roughest day.
(Act I, Scene 3)

(5) To indicate a state of mental resolution:

Blow, wind! come, wrack!
At least we'll die with harness on our back.
(Act V, Scene 5)

By having the witches speak in rhyme, Shakespeare followed his usual custom with regard to supernatural beings. The fairies in *A Midsummer Night's Dream* also speak in rhyme.

Question 15.
Ambiguity plays an important part in *Macbeth*. Describe briefly three instances in which this theme is developed.

Answer
The theme of ambiguity, or doubledealing, may be illustrated first, when the witches greet Macbeth with two prophecies. The first prophecy (that he will become thane of Cawdor) is realized almost at once and is very agreeable to Macbeth. The second (that Macbeth will become king) is achieved only after certain obstacles have been forcibly removed. Macbeth assumed that the two predictions would be equally true and agreeable, since the first was true and agreeable. He was not prepared for the second's being true, but involving such unpleasant consequences.

The second apparition tells Macbeth that "none of woman born" shall harm him, yet this ambiguous description does not rule out harm (in this case, death) by the hand of a man (Macduff) who has not been born in the usual manner ("untimely ripp'd from his mother's womb"). Macbeth's belief in his own power, as a result of this prediction, leads him to fail to see the dangerous ambiguity in the language of the prophecy.

The assurance of the third apparition, that:

> Macbeth shall never vanquish'd be until
> Great Birnam Wood to high Dunsinane Hill
> Shall come against him

is, again, misleading. The prediction seems to say that Macbeth will never be conquered, yet the wood moves — when the English troops camouflage themselves with tree branches and creep toward the castle unnoticed.

These three illustrations demonstrate how the witches "cow'd" Macbeth's reason ("my better part of man"). He sees, too late for action, that he should not have believed these "juggling fiends" that:

> palter with us in a double sense;
> That keep the word of promise to our ear,
> And break it to our hope.

Question 16.
Discuss the imagery of blood and of darkness in *Macbeth*.

Answer
An image is a word picture that appeals, in a visual manner, to the imagination. Shakespeare uses blood imagery extensively in *Macbeth*. The bleeding sergeant tells his tale of bloody execution and of soldiers who fought as though they meant "to bathe in reeking wounds." The dreadful image of Lady Macbeth praying that cruelty may so thicken her blood that pity shall not flow in her veins is even more vivid. The murderer appears at the door of the banquet hall with blood upon his face, while Banquo's corpse is described as having "twenty trenched gashes on his head" and is truly "blood-bolter'd." Macbeth gazes at his hand, which seems to dye the whole ocean red ("incarnadine"). All the perfumes of Arabia cannot wash Lady Macbeth's hands clean. She utters words that are perhaps the most horrible in the entire play: "Yet who would have thought the old man to have had so much blood in him?" Finally, Malcolm imagines Macbeth

holding a bloody sceptre. This blood imagery brings a sense of dynamic violence to the tragedy.

Night or darkness imagery also dominates much of this play. All the remarkable scenes take place during the night or in some dark spot. Thus, the dagger hallucination, Duncan's murder, Banquo's murder and Lady Macbeth's sleepwalking all happen at night. The witches dance during the darkness of the storm on the black heath. Macbeth asks that the stars hide their fires so that they may not reveal or witness his "black desires." Lady Macbeth calls on thick night to come "palled" (cloaked) in the "dunnest" (blackest) smoke of hell. Lady Macbeth, in her last appearance in the play, comes to fear the dark, since she (paradoxically) has "light by her continually."

Question 17.
Discuss the use of disease imagery in *Macbeth*.

Answer
Disease imagery occurs frequently in the latter part of *Macbeth*. The suggestion conveyed by this imagery is that Macbeth, as a usurping tyrant, is the source of an infection that spreads disease throughout Scotland, a disease that can only be cured by his removal and Malcolm's taking over the throne.

Macbeth regards life as a "fitful fever." He speaks of himself as shaken by fear and of lying in restless torment, his shivering, tossing and turning suggesting fever. His description of his mind as a torture rack and as full of scorpions can also be regarded as disease imagery — that is, imagery conveying an impression of physical illness or bodily pain.

Ross, in his dialogue with Lady Macduff, speaks of the times as feverish. Kings, both good and bad, were supposed to fashion their countries in their own image, and here we see how the feverishness of the tyrant has infected the country. Macduff, telling Malcolm of Scotland's troubles, personifies it, speaking of Scotland as wounded, bleeding, driven and sinking in weariness. A contrast is suggested between Scotland, ruled by Macbeth, and England, ruled by Edward the Confessor. Edward, the possessor of the king's touch, miraculously heals: Macbeth infects and destroys.

The doctor who appears in the scene in England comments that Edward's cures go beyond the knowledge of medical science. In the next scene, the doctor who watches Lady Macbeth revealing her sick soul comments, similarly, that her cure can only be achieved by a clergyman. Macbeth points to the parallel between Lady Macbeth and Scotland when he asks the doctor if he can do anything about the sickness of the country. The irony is that it is the moral sickness of him and Lady Macbeth that is the cause of his country's illness, and it is the English force commanded by Malcolm that will restore health to the country. The Scottish nobles going to join this force consider Malcolm the medicine for the sick country and state that they are ready to shed their blood as a healing potion for Scotland.

Question 18.
Identify and illustrate briefly two different methods by which the playwright achieves a distinctive mood or atmosphere.

Answer
In the first scene, Shakespeare wanted to create a mysterious, ominous atmosphere. One means by which he does this is characterization. What more mysterious characters could be presented to the audience than the three witches? These "midnight hags" appear on the "blasted heath" chanting their ambiguous words:

Fair is foul and foul is fair,
Hover through the fog and filthy air.

These words, which have several meanings, contribute a threatening note to this scene.

Another method by which Shakespeare creates atmosphere is through contrast. The heart-warming scene between Lady Macduff and her son forms a sharp contrast with the evil of most of the play. The gentle teasing between mother and son ("little monkey, thou speakest with all thy wit") and the childlike innocence of the boy as he speaks about traitors and "liars and swearers" makes this one of the brightest scenes in the play, creating an atmosphere of comfort, friendliness and love, which is soon destroyed by the entrance of the murderers.

Question 19.
Show how, in three important instances after his coronation, Macbeth's efforts to achieve security make his position worse.

Answer

Macbeth decides to kill Banquo and Fleance, since he believes the prophecy of the witches that Banquo will be the father of future kings. He does not trust Banquo, who, he feels, knows too much and could cause him trouble. He therefore arranges for the murder of the two, but Fleance escapes. This leaves him still disturbed by "saucy doubts and fears." Then, when Banquo's ghost appears at the banquet, Macbeth acts in such a way that he arouses the suspicions of the assembled lords. The crime has a damaging effect on both his mind and his future.

Macbeth decides to consult the witches again. Through an apparition, they advise Macbeth to beware of Macduff. Macbeth decides to kill Macduff, but before the deed can be carried out, Macduff escapes to England. In anger, Macbeth vows to kill Lady Macduff and her family. He states: "The firstlings of my heart will be the firstlings of my hand and so the deed is done." Macduff, on hearing of his family's murder, swears vengeance, and he is the man who finally kills Macbeth. Thus, Macbeth's decision makes his position worse.

During Macbeth's visit to the three witches, he is told that he can be killed only by a man not born of woman. This prediction fills him with confidence and proves to be his final downfall. He enters the fight against Macduff certain he cannot die. When Macduff tells him that he was "from his mother's womb untimely ripped," he destroys Macbeth's last hope. The witches' prophecy turns out to be deceptive and it leads Macbeth to his death.

Question 20.

Select a scene that provides a contrast with the prevailing mood of the play. Explain the contrast and its chief dramatic function.

Answer

The porter's scene provides contrast with the prevailing mood of the play. Preceding it, we have the murder of Duncan and the scene where the hysterical Macbeth refuses to carry the bloody dagger back to the room where Duncan lies dead. It is, therefore, a great contrast to hear the drunken porter comment on common situations in casual prose. His remarks about French hose and tailors seem to have little to do with this great tragedy.

One of the dramatic purposes of this scene is to provide

Macbeth and Lady Macbeth with sufficient time to prepare to face the nobles knocking at the door. It gives them (especially Macbeth) time to compose themselves so that they may avoid suspicion.

Question 21.

Describe the development of the tragedy in Macbeth himself, showing both its nature and its extent.

Answer

At the beginning of the play, Macbeth, a leading general of Scotland, conducts a loyal defence of his king against invaders and rebels. From the first, however, he is ambitious to be king, as he reacts nervously when the witches mention his fate. However, at this point, he is loyal to the king, and, while he may imagine murder, his mind rejects it: "Why, if fate will have me king, fate may crown me." He has a good reputation, as shown by his friendship with Banquo, the glowing report of the sergeant and the warm greeting he receives from the king.

Gradually, however, his ambition overcomes his finer nature. When Duncan names Malcolm prince of Cumberland, Macbeth readily decides, "That is a step/On which I must fall down, or else o'erleap,/For in my way it lies."

After Duncan has arrived at Inverness and is dining, Macbeth controls his ambition for the moment and resolves not to kill the king. The weakness of his decision is soon revealed by Lady Macbeth, who, by calling him a coward, manages to change his mind. He is shown as being indifferent to the moral consequences of his act and concerned merely with the probability of unpleasant results if his plans should fail. When Lady Macbeth assures him he will not be blamed, he praises her for her resolution and says, "Bring forth men-children only. . . ." He then proceeds to murder Duncan. From this point on, Macbeth plunges into a life of evil.

Having overcome his better nature, he has little trouble doing away with his former friend, Banquo. He does not need any encouragement from Lady Macbeth; indeed, he deliberately leaves her in ignorance of his plans.

When he has killed Banquo and has seen the witches a second time, he demonstrates the extent of his deterioration by saying that now it would be best to carry out his ruthless designs without debate. This reasoning leads him to the senseless murder of Lady Macduff and her children.

The final stage in the tragedy of Macbeth is shown in his speech after hearing of Lady Macbeth's death. He can no longer show the strong love that he revealed in his letter to her near the beginning of the play. He only says, "She should have died hereafter." He goes on to demonstrate his complete disillusionment in the soliloquy, "tomorrow and tomorrow. . . ." and in his assessment of life: "It is a tale told by an idiot . . . signifying nothing." Macbeth destroyed his soul even before his defeat at the hands of Macduff.

Question 22.
Describe the tragic development of Lady Macbeth's character after the murder of Duncan.

Answer
Shakespeare presents tragedy in the life of Lady Macbeth by showing us her mental collapse. She is quite sane and strong-willed after Duncan's murder and orders Macbeth about: "Put on your nightgown . . . to bed." However, she is not consulted by Macbeth in all the later murders, and, though she tells Macbeth, "Do not sit alone making your companions sorriest fancies," we can see that she thinks of the murders as much as Macbeth does. She has lost her control of Macbeth by the time the banquet is over, and can only tell the guests to "go at once." She is well on the road to insanity in the sleepwalking scene, and it is not long afterward that we are informed, "The queen, my lord, is dead." Shakespeare presents tragedy in Lady Macbeth by showing us her gradual loss of control over her mind.

Question 23.
"The events in a tragedy of Shakespeare are influenced by forces or circumstances greater than human."

Point out two means by which the influence of such forces or circumstances upon events is suggested in *Macbeth*.

Answer
The chant of the witches in Act I, Scene 1 — "Fair is foul, and foul is fair" — shows that they intend to upset the ordinary moral universe. Their subsequent words show that they have a

sinister interest in Macbeth. Since the witches are supernatural agents, or "instruments of darkness," they represent the first greater-than-human force to influence Macbeth. The first means by which their influence is suggested to the audience is the use of spells — that is, the strange unnatural singsong chant, rising to a shriek, associated with "midnight hags." The second means is the developing power of nemesis (retributive justice), made clear at the end of the play when Macduff, its chief instrument, reveals (by describing the unusual manner of his own birth) the falseness of Macbeth's belief that he has a "charmed life." Macbeth could not have known that the murder of the Macduff household would provide the perfect motive for revenge, or nemesis, for Macduff. This developing nemesis represents a further force beyond Macbeth's control. Nemesis, along with the trick played on Macbeth by the witches, turns out to be forces strong enough to bring down even this man of iron.

Question 24.
Discuss the theme of the nature of manhood in *Macbeth*.

Answer
What makes a true man is a theme that runs throughout *Macbeth*. For Lady Macbeth, a true man is one who sets great goals for himself and is ready to do anything to achieve these goals. Moral scruples belong only to the ordinary man, she feels, not the true man, who towers above ordinary beings. Macbeth, she says, is not without ambition, but he has too much of the "milk o' human kindness," the compassion, or ordinary make-up, that the true man should be without. He would like to achieve his goal "holily," like a saint unacquainted with practical affairs.

It is by an appeal to his manhood that Lady Macbeth influences her husband. He dares to do everything that a man should, he says, and no man dares to do more. However, his objections to murdering Duncan are swept away by Lady Macbeth's passionate courage, which drives him to say, admiringly, that she should bear only male children.

When Macbeth urges the murderers to take revenge against their supposed destroyer, Banquo, he makes a similar appeal to their manhood. Are they so "gospelled," he asks, that they will pray for the man who has ruined them? The teaching of the gospels to love one's enemies is treated by him contemptuously.

A real man will respond to injuries by taking a bloody revenge, Macbeth says.

When Macbeth sees the ghost of Banquo and reveals himself to his guests, Lady Macbeth makes use of her previous scornful methods to bring him to himself. "Are you a man?" she asks. He is a man who will face a natural danger as bravely as any other, he answers, but this supernatural visit must frighten anyone. Lady Macbeth treats the ghost as a hallucination and regards his belief in it as foolish. By the end of the scene, Macbeth has accepted her view. He resolves to become mature and manly in crime.

The irony is that, in doing so, he loses all feeling. When he hears of his wife's death, he dismisses it with the observation that she had to die sometime, and it does not matter when, life being meaningless and futile. This attitude contrasts with the way in which Macduff receives the news of the death of his wife and children. He is overcome with grief, and when Malcolm urges him to bear it as a man, he answers that he must also feel it as a man. Tender feelings are as much a part of manhood as anger and courage. Macduff has both and he converts his grief into the anger that he uses to take revenge on Macbeth.